The Syntax of Negation in Russian

in Russian

T0345316

STANFORD MONOGRAPHS IN LINGUISTICS

THE SYNTAX OF NEGATION
IN RUSSIAN
A Minimalist Approach

Sue Brown

CSLI
PUBLICATIONS
Center for the Study of
Language and Information
Stanford, California

Library of Congress Cataloging-in-Publication Data

Brown, Sue, 1967–
The syntax of negation in Russian : a minimalist approach / Sue Brown.
p.   cm. — (Stanford monographs in linguistics)
Includes bibliographical references and index.

ISBN 1-57586-168-2 (pa. : alk. paper).
ISBN 1-57586-169-0 (cl. : alk. paper)

1. Russian language—Negatives. I. Title. II. Series.
PG2359.N4B76   1999
491.75—dc21   99-18173
CIP

∞ The acid-free paper used in this book meets the minimum requirements of the American National Standard for Information Sciences—Permanence of Paper for Printed Library Materials, ANSI Z39.48-1984.

in memory of Hayley

Table of Contents

Preface

This monograph is a thoroughly revised version of my 1996 Indiana University doctoral dissertation *The Syntax of Negation in Russian*. The overall structure remains the same. However, the actual analyses have been supplemented, modified, updated, and streamlined significantly. Chapter 1 of the dissertation has been split into two separate chapters, one devoted to the phenomena discussed in this monograph and one devoted to an overview of the Minimalist Program (Chomsky 1995), the framework within which the analysis is written. The most important revisions include the elimination of the use of the Negative Operator. In the dissertation the analysis relied on the presence of a negative operator in earlier chapters, which was replaced with a negative feature in later chapters. In this monograph I employ the negative feature throughout, which makes the presentation herein substantially more consistent. In addition, the superfluous analysis of Negative Concord in Russian within the Government and Binding Framework (Chomsky 1982) has been eliminated. Instead I present a Minimalist analysis throughout the monograph. Finally, detailed presentations of earlier work on the subject, which are the hallmark of any dissertation, have been abbreviated. Of course, I have retained those discussions in full, where they are germane to the analysis at hand.

Of all the people who helped me in this work, I would like to thank Steven Franks and Laurent Dekydstpotter for countless hours of discussion, helpful comments, and for setting a good example for me to follow. For other discussion, comments, and/or correspondence related to this work or previous versions of it, I am also grateful to Linda Schwartz, Ljiljana Progovac, George Fowler, Ronald Feldstein, Chris Collins, Wayne Harbert, Wayles Browne, John Bailyn, Tracy King, Javier Martin-Gonzales, Kylie Skewes, Elizabeth Thompson, Dominika Baran, and, especially, Željko Bošković, who took the time to read through both the dissertation and the manuscript for this monograph and provide pages of extensive comments. For native speaker judgments, I am forever indebted to Kris Pridanov, Galina McClaws, Vadim Liapunov, Nina Perlina, Anna Shparberg, Natasha Borovikova, Marina Kanevskaya, Vladimir Gitin, and Julia Vaingurt.

Research for previous versions of this work was presented in seminars given at Harvard University. I would like to thank the Slavic Department at Harvard for allowing me to offer these seminars, and for the wonderful students of those seminars for being interested in my work and for truly insightful and thought provoking discussions. In addition, some material in this work was presented in various forms at talks given at Indiana University and Harvard University, and in papers given at the 1996 meeting of the *American Association of Teachers of Slavic and East European Languages*, at the 1995 meeting of the *Formal Linguistics Society of Mid-America*, and at *Formal Approaches to Slavic Linguistics* IV, V, and VII. I would like the thank the audiences of those talks and papers for helpful and thoughtful comments and discussion. Some of the material in this work has appeared elsewhere in published form in various guises, as referenced in the monograph, including Brown 1995 and Brown and Franks 1995. I would like the thank the anonymous reviewers of Brown and Franks 1995 for helpful discussion.

I would also like to express my most heartfelt thanks to my research assistant Kylie Skewes, who was instrumental in preparing the camera-ready copy of this manuscript. Of course, any editorial glitches are my sole responsibility.

Finally, I would like to thank Vince for his undying support and love throughout, and my family for all they have done for me through the years. Without them, this book would not have been written.

Some of the research presented here was funded by a grant from the Mellon Foundation and Indiana University's Russian and East European Institute.

Chapter 1: Negation Phenomena in Russian

1.0. Introduction

The majority of the foremost work on negation in generative syntax has focused on its behavior in the West Germanic, Romance, and Asian languages (cf. Ladusaw 1992, Zanuttini 1991, Laka 1990, Haegeman 1995, among others). Some work has been done on Serbian/Croatian as a representative of the Slavic group (cf. Progovac 1988, 1991, 1992b, 1992c, 1993a, 1993b, 1993c, 1993d, 1994), but the picture provided for Slavic by Serbian/Croatian is incomplete. In this work I hope to contribute further insights from another representative of the Slavic language family, namely Russian, to the current lively discussion of negation in the literature.

1.1. Negation Phenomena in Russian

Russian displays two generally assumed diagnostics for clausal negation: morphologically negative constituents (henceforth, **NI-words**) which are licensed in and only in the scope of overt clausemate negation; and the language-specific **Genitive of Negation**, the optional Case-marking of the internal argument of a negated verb. These diagnostics contrast in striking ways.

1

Russian NI-words, which consist of the negative particle *ni* attached to a WH-element, obligatorily cooccur with the sentential negation marker *ne*, regardless of their thematic role or configuration, as shown in (1).[1]

(1) **Nikto nikogda nigde   ni s   kem** *(ne) tancuet.[2]

    no-who no-when no-where no with who NEG dances

    'No one ever dances anywhere with anyone.'

In other words, the NI-words exhibit **Negative Concord** (NC). NC refers to the cooccurrence of multiple negative constituents expressing a single instance of negation. This pattern differs from the languages discussed in the literature on NC. For example, in West Flemish, negative constituents *must* occur in a specific configuration with respect to the morphological indicator of sentential negation in order to receive a NC interpretation. Otherwise they receive an interpretation of **Double Negation** (DN), i.e., the negative constituents cancel each other out (cf. Haegeman 1995). Standard English never exhibits NC and disallows the cooccurrence of negative constituents, except with DN readings, while familiar non-standard dialects allow it. Italian and Spanish disallow the cooccurrence of preverbal negative constituents with a sentential negation marker, while postverbal ones require it; Catalan displays a similar pattern, except the negative marker can optionally cooccur with a preverbal negative constituent (cf. Ladusaw 1992, Haegeman 1995, Laka 1990, Zanuttini 1991, 1997, Vallduví 1994). An interesting fact about earlier stages of Russian that I will return to in Section 3.5 is that Old Russian (and Old Church Slavonic) behaves like Catalan. In other words, the negative marker *ne* can optionally cooccur with preverbal negative constituents, while its occurrence is obligatory (always attested) with postverbal ones. This latter pattern also occurs in Russian dialects (Borkovksij and Kuznecov 1965: 439-441).

Genitive of Negation (GN) refers to the optional Genitive Case-marking of Noun Phrases (NPs) that enter a syntactic derivation in a negated verb's internal argument position. It is widely assumed that GN requires clausemate sentential negation in order to occur (Babby 1980a, 1980b, Bailyn 1997, among many others). Despite this, the occurrence of Genitive of Negation with clausemate sentential negation, unlike the NI-words, is distributionally restricted. The examples below show that environments for GN include direct objects of transitive verbs (2), and subjects of unaccusative intransitive verbs (3), but not subjects of unergative intransitive verbs (4) or

---

[1] Note that the particle *ni* can also occur on non-pronominal NPs as in (i).

(i) On **ne** čital **n i** odnoj knigi.

    he NEG read not one book

    'He didn't read a single book.'

I will refer to such constituents in the text as NI-words as well.

[2] When a negative pronoun occurs as the object of a preposition, the preposition splits the morpheme *ni* from the WH-element.

transitive verbs (5). Nouns inherently Case-marked with one of Russian's other cases likewise are not candidates for GN (6):[3]

(2) Rita **ne** pišet **statej/stat'i**.

Rita NEG writes articles$_{GEN}$/articles$_{ACC}$

'Rita doesn't write articles.'

Modified from Strugackij and Strugackij 1993

(3) a. **Otveta** **ne** prišlo.

answer$_{GEN}$ NEG came$_{NEUT, SG}$

'No answer came.'

b. **Otvet** **ne** prišel

answer$_{NOM}$ NEG came$_{MASC, SG}$

'The answer didn't come.'

(4) *__Lingvistov__ ne spit/spjat[4]

linguists$_{GEN}$ NEG sleep$_{3RD,SG/3RD,PL}$

(5) *__Studentov__ ne čitaet/čitajut stixi.

students$_{GEN}$ NEG read$_{3RD,SG/3RD,PL}$ poems

(6) Ja **ne** zvonila **moej sestre/*moej sestry**.

I NEG called my sister$_{DAT}$/my sister$_{GEN}$

'I didn't call my sister.'

In addition to this distributional contrast, NI-words and GN exhibit asymmetric behavior in contexts of **expletive negation** (cf. Grevisse 1988, Espinal 1991, 1992, Brown and Franks 1995, 1997, Brown 1995b, 1996a, 1996b). **Expletive negation** refers to instances of formal sentential negation containing a sentential negation marker but carrying no negative force. The canonical cases of expletive negation occur in fixed lexical expressions. Their lack of negative force is evident in the semantic interpretation of the clause containing them. This type of lexical expletive negation occurs in Russian with a number of expressions, such as *čut' ne* ('almost'), *poka ne* ('until'), and in subordinate clauses marked with the conditional introduced by the conjunctions *kak by* and *čtoby* after expressions of fear and worry.

---

[3] I repeat here that Genitive Case marking on any argument where it can occur is optional. Direct objects of negated transitive verbs may also be marked with Accusative Case; subjects of negated unaccusative verbs may also be marked with Nominative Case.

[4] I include both forms of the verb to show that it is not the lack of subject verb agreement that causes (4) to be ungrammatical.

Expletive negation cannot license NI-words, as may be expected, but, surprisingly, it does license GN, as shown in (7) from Mustajoki 1985, where the NI-word *nikto* 'no one' is disallowed, while GN marking of the direct object *èksperimenta* 'experiment' is fine. In place of the NI-word *nikto*, an indefinite in *-nibud'*, not capable of freely occurring in the scope of clausemate negation, is required.

(7) On boitsja, kak by   **kto-nibud'/*nikto ne**   narušil

 he fears, how MOD who-any/ no-who NEG ruin$_{COND}$

 èksperimenta.

 experiment$_{GEN}$

 'He's afraid someone/*no one might ruin the experiment.'

In order to negate the embedded clause in (7), a negated indicative clause without the conjunction *kak by* is necessary, as shown in (8). Here the NI-word is not only allowed, it is required. Of course, GN is still fine.

(8) On boitsja, čto **nikto/ *kto-nibud' ne**   narušit

 he fears that no-who who-any NEG ruin$_{FUT}$

 èksperimenta.

 experiment$_{GEN}$

 'He's afraid no one will ruin the experiment (i.e., he wants someone to ruin it).'

Along with these instances of lexical expletive negation, negation that occurs in certain types of Yes/No questions exhibits this same strange pattern with respect to the occurrence of the NI-words and GN. These include negated Yes/No questions with the second-position interrogative clitic *li*. In such questions, the verb, hosting negation, which is also a clitic, moves to sentence-initial position to host *li*. We see from example (9) that negation in these questions also fails to license the NI-words, but does license GN.

(9) [$_{CP}$ [$_C$ [**Ne** vyzyvaet] [$_C$ **li**]] [$_{TP}$ tol'ko pobeda kadetov

   NEG cause   Q   only victory of-cadets

 kakix-nibud'/ *nikakix besporjadkov]]?

 [which-some/ no-which disturbances]$_{GEN}$

 'Could it be that the cadet victory is causing some disturbances?'

In (9) the NI-word *nikakix* is disallowed, but GN-marking on *kakix-nibud' besporjadkov* is fine.[5]

---

[5] Note that the *nibud'*-pronoun itself is allowed here as well (cf. (7))

1.2. Outline

The analysis that follows of the negation phenomena presented above is couched in the framework of the most recently published version of the Minimalist Program (Chomsky 1995). In Chapter 2, I present its most relevant aspects. In Chapter 3, I propose a Minimalist account of the distribution and syntactic behavior of the NI-words. In Chapter 4, I analyze the Genitive of Negation and compare its distribution with that of NI-words discussed in Chapter 3. I first develop a structural account of Genitive of Negation (GN). I then turn to a Minimalist analysis of the syntactic mechanisms that determine GN Case marking, which can be extended to other grammatical Cases in Russian as well as to Case marking in other languages. The conclusions reached in Chapters 3 and 4 will form the basis for the discussion of expletive negation in lexical contexts and Yes/No questions to be developed in Chapter 5. Chapter 6 is devoted to a formalization of the status of negation within the phrase structure of Russian and to its importance in understanding the universal syntactic expression of negation. This account will contribute relevant Slavic data to the pool of negation data and shed new light on the syntactic expression of negation universally.

Chapter 2: The Minimalist Program

2.0. Introduction

Chomsky's recent work developing a minimalist approach to the study of language has led to radical reformulations of many theories that were long considered standard (but not unquestioned) in generative grammar. In this chapter I make no claims to present the history of generative grammar from its earliest days, nor to present a thorough critique of the direction of its development at any stage. For those interested in reviewing earlier versions from Standard Theory to Revised Extended Standard Theory to Government and Binding Theory to Principles and Parameters Theory, I suggest Radford 1981, 1988, Lasnik and Uriagereka 1988, Chomsky 1995, Haegeman 1995, or Hornstein 1995, and more recently Radford 1997, all of which contain fairly in-depth discussions of the development of generative grammar at the time the books were written.

Minimalism adopts an earlier goal of the theory of language, which was to explain why syntactic objects appear in speech in positions "displaced" from where they are interpreted. The assumption is that this property "should be reduced to morphology-driven movement (Chomsky 1995: 222)." For this reason, syntactic derivations converge only when movement which is absolutely necessary has taken place in order to check certain morphological features. The Minimalist program strives to create a model of language that eliminates unnecessary steps in the representation of the derivation of a sentence. As Chomsky notes, the "guiding intuition of the Minimalist Program is that operations apply anywhere, without special stipulation, the derivation crashing if a 'wrong choice' is made (1995: 231)." Some of the most important basic premises of the Minimalist Program are outlined in the following subsections.

2.1. The Computational Component

In the Minimalist framework, the Revised Extended Standard Theory (REST) multi-level model of derivation from D(eep)-Structure to the levels of Logical Form (LF) and Phonological Form (PF) via S(urface)-Structure, illustrated in (1), disappears.

(1)   Model of Derivation from REST (Chomsky 1972)

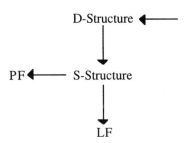

According to the Minimalist program the operations of the computational system of human language recursively construct *syntactic objects* from items listed in a numeration and from syntactic objects already formed (Chomsky 1995: 226). The term *numeration* refers to an *array* of items that can potentially be joined to form a larger syntactic object and ultimately a convergent sentence. Chomsky defines the numeration as "a set of pairs (LI, *i*), where LI is an item of the lexicon and *i* is its index, understood to be the number of times that LI is selected" to be included in a given derivation. Syntactic objects are recursively built from the items in the numeration and syntactic objects already formed by operations known as **Select** and **Merge** (cf. Chomsky 1995: 226). Select chooses a lexical item from the numeration and introduces it into the derivation. Merge combines the newly selected lexical items with syntactic objects already formed to create a new syntactic object. The derivation converges when these two operations have exhausted all the items listed in the original numeration. The computational system of human language in creating syntactic objects from the numeration, maps the numeration onto the only two interfaces allowed for in the Minimalist program: the articulatory-perceptual (PF) and conceptual-intentional (LF) interfaces. The levels known as D-Structure and S-Structure are eliminated.

2.2. Types of Features

Within the computational component of human language, the notion of feature checking drives movement of constituents. Feature checking is reduced more or less to feature deletion, whereby a "checked feature is marked 'invisible at the interface' (Chomsky 1995: 229)." It is assumed that different types of features have different degrees of applicability for the different interface levels PF and LF. According to Chomsky:

> We assume, then, that at some point in the (uniform) computation to LF, there is an operation Spell-Out that applies to the structure Σ already formed. Spell-Out strips away from Σ those elements relevant only to π [the phonological component], leaving the residue Σ_L, which is mapped to λ [the LF component] by operations of the kind used to form Σ. Σ itself is then mapped to π by operations unlike those of the N[umeration] $\rightarrow$ λ computation. We call the subsystem of C_{HL} that maps Σ to π the *phonological component*, and subsystem that continues the computation from Σ_L to LF the *covert component*. The pre-Spell-Out computation we call *overt*.
> Chomsky 1995: 229

Hence, a lexical item will contain two types of features: those relevant for PF and those relevant for LF. The types of features relevant only for LF, i.e., accessible to the computation, include **formal** features such as [±V(erb)], [±N(oun)], and [±plural], but not purely **semantic** features such as [+human] (Chomsky's feature). Some features that are relevant for LF are **intrinsic**; these include the categorial features ([±N], [±V], etc...), Case-checking features of the verb (or preposition), person features ([1st], [2nd], [3rd]), and gender features ([MASC], [NEUT], [FEM]).[1] Others are **optional** in a way to be made clear shortly. These include Case features (e.g. [NOM], [ACC], [DAT]) and number features ([SING], [DUAL], [PLURAL]). Functional categories, such as Tense, Complementizer, and Determiner, also have formal properties, and in some cases phonological properties as well.

Within this framework, certain formal features are **strong**, and force overt movement in spite of Procrastinate (overt movement being more costly/less economical than covert movement). For Chomsky the strong features are those that a derivation simply "cannot tolerate" and which trigger rules that eliminate them: "[strength] is associated with a pair of operations, one that introduces it into the derivation (actually, a combination of Select and Merge), a second that (quickly) eliminates it (1995: 233)." An example of a strong feature is the [D(eterminer)] feature of I(nflection) or T(ense) which induces overt raising of a DP to Subj position;

---

[1] Željko Bošković (personal communication) points out that might be better to divide features into phonological, semantic, and formal, since certain formal features, i.e., categorial features, are clearly needed in phonology (e.g., to determine stress).

this basically serves as a Minimalist interpretation of the Extended Projection Principle (EPP) which requires all sentences to have subjects.

In order for a derivation to converge, it must meet the condition of **Full Interpretation**. This principle states that no uninterpretable element can remain at the point where the derivation enters the semantic component. These uninterpretable, or –Interpretable, elements include the strong features just discussed, as well as Case features of nouns and pronominal features, or so-called "Φ-features", of the verb. Such features must be erased by the checking operation in order for a derivation to converge. I will return to a more detailed discussion of [±Interpretable] features in the discussion of Checking Theory in Section 2.4.

One aspect of the theory of features within the Minimalist program is of particular importance for this study, especially for the account of Genitive of Negation in Chapter 4. This is the mechanism by which certain lexical items obtain the features that play a role in computation. It has often been assumed that lexical items are inserted from the lexicon into the derivation with features present and that some of these features, e.g., Case and Agreement features, are automatically determined by the lexical item's base configuration. For example, the DP that occupies the complement–to–V position will be inserted from the lexicon with its Acc Case features already present. Within the more recent framework, no such stipulation is made. It is assumed in this monograph, along with Chomsky (1995: 237), that "Case and Φ-features are added arbitrarily as a noun [or verb] is selected for the numeration [from the lexicon]." In other words, any Case-marked DP can be inserted into any position, and independent principles will conspire to prevent illegitimate structures from converging. This will be important when we discuss the mechanisms that mark Genitive of Negation in Section 4.6.

2.3. The Architecture of the System

Under Minimalist assumptions, the rigid notions of X-bar phrase structure theory, that sought to eliminate the more random phrase structure rules from the grammar, are discarded in favor of a sort of "free-choice" sentence formation. In earlier versions of X-bar theory, each (minimal) head X° would project a maximal projection XP containing a Specifier, a Complement, and an intermediate projection X', as shown in (2):

(2)   XP projection of the head X^0

In (2) the head X^0 projects to the maximal (XP) level as shown.

In the Minimalist program X-bar theory is eliminated. Derivations are viewed as a series of the operations Select and Merge followed by Attract/Move, all of which are restricted by Minimalist principles aimed at determining the least "costly" derivation in terms of computation. XP and X^0 no longer exist *per se*, nor does X', although these labels continue to be used for the sake of convenience. In this new "Bare Phrase Structure", according to Chomsky (1995: 228), languages are subject to a condition of inclusiveness which is formulated as follows:

> ...any structure formed by the computation...is constituted of elements already present in the lexical items selected for N [the numeration]; no new objects are added in the course of computation apart from rearrangements of lexical properties (in particular, no indices, bar levels in the sense of X-bar theory, etc.)

With reference to the categories of Bare Phrase Structure, Chomsky (1995: 249) says that:

> ...categories are elementary constructions from properties of lexical items, satisfying the inclusiveness condition (cf. above); there are no bar levels and no distinction between lexical items and "heads" projected from them (cf. 3b). A consequence is that an item can be both an X^0 and an XP.

Thus the standard X-bar structure of (3a), where *the* and *book* are terminal lexical items and D+ and N+ represent the properties of these items relevant for computation, is replaced by the structure in (3b) (Chomsky 1995: 246).

(3) a. Standard X-bar Structure

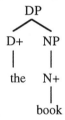

b. Bare Phrase Structure

As shown here, in Bare Phrase Structure there actually is no distinction between terminal and non-terminal elements; all projections are the lexical items themselves. Any category that projects no further is a maximal projection (XP or X^{min}) and one that does not project at all is a minimal projection (X^{min}); any other category is the equivalent of X' and is invisible at the interface and for computation. For this reason a head that projects no further can be considered a maximal projection, and Specs and Complements are no longer fixed elements of a projection. Heads in this sense are understood to be the "terminal elements" drawn from the lexicon, and the notions specifier and complement are understood as relations to the head in the same way as in the earlier theory. The label X^0 now refers to a zero-level category, which includes a head or a category formed by adjunction to a head that projects. Categories which are formed by adjunction to a head, such as the head T(ense) with V adjoined, are referred to as X^{0max}, as in (4), where Y^0 is adjoined to X^0.

(4)   Structure of X^{0max}

As mentioned before, structure building is carried out by the operations Select, Merge, and Attract/Move, the latter being driven by feature checking requirements. The operations Merge and Attract/Move involve both adjunction and substitution. Adjunction forms a two-segment category, while substitution forms a new category. Adjunction is understood in much the same way as in traditional generative literature, while substitution actually refers to the process of creating a new category by adding a Specifier to a head that is targeted for a given operation. Categories in Bare Phrase Structure are labeled according to the types of structures created by these two processes. It is still possible to continue to refer to these structure with the traditional X-bar labels, but to understand them purely as labels, and not categories in and of themselves.

2.4. Checking Theory

As mentioned above, movement in the Minimalist program is driven by morphological feature checking: some feature must be checked in order for movement to take place. By the principle of Full Interpretation, in order for a derivation to be computable, it must not contain certain inaccessible elements. These include unchecked (hence, unerased) [–Interpretable] features, including strong features. Features are checked by entering into a checking relation with a targeted element's sublabel, or list of features, in one of three configurations, as shown in (5). The checking domain is created by adjunction to an XP or head, or substitution (which creates a Spec position).

(5)   *Feature Checking*

(a)   **Creation of a Specifier Position (Substitution):** A YP (maximal projection) raises to create a checking configuration with an

X^0 that has the appropriate feature in its feature sublabel (matrix). X^0 projects and a new projection XP = [YP X'] is created.

(b)   **Adjunction to XP** (a two-segment XP is created): A YP (maximal projection) raises to adjoin to a maximal projection (which can consist of a non-projecting head); a two-segment XP is created.

(c)   **Adjunction to X^0** (new zero-level maximal projection is created): A head Y^0 (or its non-overt feature sublabel) raises to adjoin to a head X^0; this is the only option for covert raising of features.

From these configurations (cf. especially (5c)) we see that movement for checking in the most recent version of the Minimalist program is not limited to overt elements. Features themselves can raise covertly to check a feature of the sublabel of the targeted element. In fact, following recent assumptions, this is the standard operation. Overt raising takes place as a form of pied-piping, in which the feature that raises carries along with it only whatever overt material is necessary for PF convergence. What is obligatorily pied-piped is the entire (non-overt) feature sublabel. A feature F (and whatever overt material is necessary for convergence) raises by Move F, if it is unchecked, taking along the feature sublabel, and it enters into one of the checking relations outlined in (5) (cf. Chomsky 1995: 266, n. 29); a checking relation is possible only if the target has a feature that has not been checked yet. The feature to be checked can either be on the head of the target itself, or on some element that is adjoined to the head. The other features in the sublabel go along as "free riders", and these features may also enter into checking relations with features in the sublabel of the target.

As mentioned in Section 2.2, there are various types of intrinsic and optional features. However, as Chomsky notes (1995: 277), the distinction between intrinsic and optional features is relatively unimportant, compared to the distinction between features which enter into interpretation at LF and those which are uninterpretable and must be eliminated by the principle of Full Interpretation. Interpretable features include the Φ-features of nouns and the categorial features [V], [N], etc...; all others, including the Case features of nouns, features that indicate that an affix is required, Case-assigning features of T and V, as well as the Φ-features of verbs and adjectives are considered [–Interpretable]. Within Checking Theory, the feature of the target of movement that enters into a checking relation is always [–Interpretable], i.e., needs to be checked and erased, while the feature of the moved item can be either [±Interpretable] . For example, the [–Interpretable] Φ-features of the verb need to be checked, and are checked by the [+Interpretable] Φ-features of the Subj. Therefore, any type of feature can occur in a **checking domain**, but need not necessarily enter into a **checking relation**.

Within earlier versions of Checking Theory, checking was understood as deletion. Checked features were deleted, remaining accessible to the computational system, while being invisible at LF. In the most recent versions, it is recognized that some features are checked but not deleted, i.e., the [+Interpretable] features, like the Φ-features of the noun, while others are unavailable even to the computational system after being checked, hence deleted *and* erased. Chomsky provides the following generalization (1995: 279):

(6) a. Features visible at LF are accessible to the computation C_{HL} throughout, whether checked or not.

b. Features invisible at LF are inaccessible to C_{HL} once checked.

Hence entering a checking relation does not obligatorily mean that a feature will be deleted and erased. Chomsky claims that a checked feature is deleted when possible and that a deleted feature is erased when possible (1995: 280, n. 52). Interpretable features are not deleted, because they cannot be; they are necessary to the computation. [–Interpretable] features are deleted and erased, once checked, unless some parametric property requires the deleted feature, which is still accessible to the computation, but invisible at LF, to postpone erasure as long as possible, perhaps to allow multiple feature checking (cf. Chomsky 1995, Section 4.5.2).

2.5. Feature Mismatch

Of significant importance for the current study, especially the chapters on Genitive of Negation and on negated Yes/No questions, is what happens when two mismatching features occur in the same checking domain.

Intuitively we predict this to block the derivation in some way, as is claimed by Chomsky (1995: 309).

(7)   Mismatch of features cancels the derivation.

Chomsky states that "the point here is literally to bar alternatives....If the optimal derivation creates a mismatch, we are not permitted to pursue a nonoptimal alternative (1995: 309)." This requires the additional modification to the notion "Checking" relation" in (8) (1995: 310).

(8)   Feature F' of FF[F] [a sublabel of features for a given item] is in a *checking configuration* with *f*; and F' is in a *checking relation* with *f* if, furthermore, F' and *f* match.

Chomsky provides the following illustration (1995: 310) with respect to Case assignment to the Subj DP, noting the distinction between checking configuration and checking relation:

> In the illustrative example, if DP has nonnominative Case and has been raised to [Spec, T], the Case feature [CF] of DP is in a checking configuration with the Case feature of T, but not in a checking relation with it. Hence, the target TP did not attract [CF], because no checking relation is established. It does, however, attract the categorial feature [D] of DP, to satisfy the EPP. But then [CF] is in a mismatching checking configuration with *f*, and the derivation is canceled.

Note that non-matching features are invisible for purposes of Attract/Move.

> Suppose that *f* is the Case-assigning feature of K, α and β have the unchecked Case features F_α and F_β (respectively), and F_α but not F_β matches *f*. Suppose that β is closer to K than α. Does β prevent K from attracting α? The Case feature F_β of β does not do so; it is not attracted by K and is therefore no more relevant than some semantic feature of β. Suppose, however, that β has some other feature F'_β that *can* enter into a checking relation with a sublabel of K. Then β is attracted by K, which cannot "see" the more remote element α. A mismatching relation is created, and the derivation is canceled: α cannot be attracted.

I will return to the relevance of this in Chapters 4 and 5.

2.6. Constraints on Movement and the operation Attract

As noted above, the operation Move F takes place in order to check features. This operation creates a chain of the form $(\alpha, t(\alpha))$, where $t(\alpha)$ is the trace left by the moved element α. Move F is subject to various constraints, one of them being the principle of Last Resort (9), which allows movement only when necessary to check features.

(9)   *Last Resort* (Chomsky 1995: 280, n. 51)

Move F raises F to target K only if F enters into a checking relation with a sublabel of K.

Another is the Minimal Link Condition (MLC), which is reminiscent of the notion of "shortest move". About this condition Chomsky states (1995: 297):

> The formulation of the MLC is more natural if we reinterpret the operation of movement as "attraction": instead of thinking of α as raising to target K, let us think of K as attracting the closest appropriate α. We define *Attract F* in terms of the condition (10), incorporating the MLC and Last Resort (understood as in (9))
>
> (10) K *attracts* F if F is the closest feature that can enter into a checking relation with a sublabel of K.
>
> If K attracts F, then α merges with K and enters its checking domain, where α is the minimal element including FF[F] [the feature sublabel] that allows convergence: FF[F] alone if the operation is covert. The operation forms the chain (α, t).

The notion "equidistance" plays a role in the MLC, which hinges on the concept of "closeness". In the most recent version of Minimalism, this notion is at first slightly modified to accommodate the fact that features now raise covertly for checking. "Closeness" is defined as in (11) (Chomsky 1995: 355).

(11) β is *closer to* HP than α if β c-commands α and is not in the minimal domain of CH, where CH is the chain headed by γ, γ adjoined within the zero-level projection $H(K)^{0max}$.

The minimal domain of CH (= chain), as defined in (12), determines a "neighborhood of H" that can be ignored in determining whether a feature F is attracted by HP (cf. Chomsky 1995: 299) for further discussion of minimal domain). Here α is a feature of an X^0 category, and CH is either the chain (α, t) or the trivial chain α.

(12)   a.   Max (α) is the smallest maximal projection including α.

      b.   The *domain* δ (CH) of CH is the set of categories included in Max (α) that are distinct from and do not contain α or t.

      c.   The *minimal domain* Min (δ (CH)) of CH is the smallest subset K of δ (CH) such that for any $\gamma \in \delta$ (CH), some $\beta \in K$ reflexively dominates γ.

However, given the Minimalist assumptions that only the head and the tail of the chain $(\alpha, t(\alpha))$ count for Attract/Move F, and not any intermediate traces, the notion of "closeness" is taken a step further and excludes non-trivial chains from the account of equidistance.

    Equidistance is thus defined as in (13) and *closeness* as in (14) (Chomsky 1995: 356):

(13) Equidistance

γ and β are equidistant from α if γ and β are in the same minimal domain.

(14) Closeness

β is *closer to* K than α unless β is in the same minimal domain as (a) τ or (b) α,

where β c-commands α and τ is the target of raising. Thus in (15), the two Spec positions are equidistant from an α = Obj in ZP.

(15)

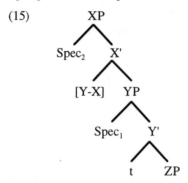

Here *t* is the trace of Y which has raised to adjoin to X. Both $Spec_2$ and $Spec_1$ are equidistant from any α in ZP or α = ZP. In other words, $Spec_1$ does not prohibit an α in ZP (or ZP itself) from targeting $Spec_2$ (substituting to create XP).

2.7. Movement and the Visibility of Traces

Another concept of the Minimalist Program that is important for the present study is that intermediate traces are invisible at LF; only the chain (α, *t*(α)) is visible for interpretation, where α is the item that has risen to the highest possible position and *t* is in the base position, i.e., the position of lexical insertion (Chomsky 1995: 301). For this reason, intermediate traces do not play a role in Move/Attract F, nor do they enter into the determination of such notions as closeness and equidistance. This is described by Chomsky (1995: 301–304) as in (16) and (17).

(16) The intermediate trace *t* of an argument cannot be attracted; hence, *t* does not prevent attraction of an element that it c-commands.

(17) Only the head of a chain CH enters into the operation Attract/Move.

2.8. Conclusion

In this chapter I have outlined the basic assumptions of the Minimalist Program that will be relevant throughout the remainder of this book. I will make constant reference to various sections throughout. In the next chapter I turn to a Minimalist account of the pattern of negative constituents, the NI-words, in Russian.

Chapter 3: Negative Constituents in Russian

3.0. Introduction

In this chapter I propose a Minimalist account of the pattern of negative constituents in Russian. I will show how a single negative feature [NEG] introduced into the derivation as the head of the functional category NegP can account for a wide array of facts, including the patterns observed for multiple occurrences of negative constituents in other languages. I argue that the substantive elements in Russian (and by extension other languages that behave similarly) that exhibit overt negative morphology have a [–Interpretable] [NEG] feature in their sublabel that is "attracted" by the [NEG] feature in NegP and checked. For this reason, the [NEG] feature of the negative constituent is checked and erased, leaving the [Interpretable] abstract feature [NEG] as the sole "expressor of negation".

3.1. Negative Concord in Russian and other Languages

As mentioned in Chapter 1, Russian displays two familiar diagnostics for clausal negation—the NI-words and Genitive of Negation—which contrast in some striking ways. In this chapter I discuss and analyze the distribution of NI-words.

The NI-words in Russian are formed by adding the negative prefix *ni-* to a K-element (i.e., WH-element), as shown in Table (1):

(1)   Formation of Russian Negative Constituents

K-element	NI-word	K-element	NI-word
kto 'who'	*nikto* 'no one'	*gde* 'where'	*nigde* 'nowhere'
čto 'what'	*ničto* 'nothing'	*kuda* 'to where'	*nikuda* 'to nowhere'
kakoj 'which'	*nikakoj* 'no such'	*kogda* 'when'	*nikogda* 'never'

Russian negative constituents require overt clausemate negation in the form of the negative verbal proclitic *ne* in order to be grammatical, as in (2):

(2)   Ivan **nigde**   **ni** s   **kem** *(**ne**) tancuet.

Ivan no-where no with who NEG dances

'Ivan doesn't dance anywhere with anyone.'

In addition, as is also seen in (2), negative pronouns in Russian exhibit **Negative Concord** (NC); NC refers to the phenomenon of multiple negative constituents expressing only one instance of negation. Thus while Standard English allows only one morphologically negative word per negated clause (cf. gloss to (2)), in languages exhibiting NC, like Russian, multiple constituents within a single negated clause can exhibit negative morphology. Nonetheless, such negated sentences are interpreted semantically as having only one instance of negation. Replacing the English non-negative indefinites in the gloss to (2) with the corresponding negative pronouns results in a reading of **Double Negation** (DN), as shown in (3):

(3)   'Ivan doesn't dance nowhere with no one.'

This sentence is grammatical in Standard English, if it is true that Ivan does dance somewhere with someone. Hence, in DN languages the multiple negative pronouns in effect cancel each other out. In familiar non-standard dialects of English, this sentence, like its Russian counterpart, would have a reading of Negative Concord.

While the unifying characteristic of languages that exhibit NC is the possible cooccurrence in negated sentences of multiple pronouns exhibiting negative morphology, the pattern of NC in Slavic differs somewhat from the pattern found in the languages that have been the focus of recent studies of negation (cf. Zanuttini 1991, Laka 1990, Haegeman and Zanuttini 1991, Progovac 1994, Zanuttini 1994, and Haegeman 1995). As mentioned above with respect to (2), negative pronouns in Slavic can only occur when the preverbal negative clitic *ne* indicating sentential negation is present in the clause. This pattern differs from the NC pattern observed in Italian, Spanish, and Catalan, discussed by Haegeman (1995) and others, where only postverbal constituents, including postposed subjects, cooccur with (and require) the negative particle; preposed negative constituents and preverbal negative subjects do not (and cannot for Italian and Spanish). The examples in (4) illustrate the contrast in Italian between sentences containing a preverbal negative subject (4a) (from Ladusaw 1992), which does not cooccur with the particle *non*, and a postverbal negative object (4b) (from Haegeman 1995), which requires it.[1]

(4)   a.   **Nessuno** (***non***) ha telefonato.

no one   not   has called

'No one called.'

   b.   Gianni *(**non**) dice **niente** a **nessuno**.

Gianni   not   said nothing to no one

'Gianni doesn't tell anyone anything.'

A further distinction of the NC pattern in Slavic is that word order permutations do not induce readings of Double Negation, whereby the negative elements cancel each other out. This pattern is attributed by Haegeman (1995) to West Flemish. According to Haegeman, in order for a NC reading to obtain in West Flemish, the negative pronoun must occur in a Spec-head relation with the negative head *nie* at S-Structure. This contrast is shown between (5a), which exhibits Negative Concord and where *van niemand* and *nie* occur in a Spec-head relation, and (5b), where they do not and which, as a result, has a reading of Double Negation.

(5)   a.   da   Valère **vanniemand nie** ketent   (en)-was

that Valère of no one   not contented **en**-was

'that Valère was not pleased with anyone' (*DN, NC)

   b.   da   Valère **nie** ketent   **vanniemand** (en)-was

that Valère not contented of   no one   **en**-was

'that Valère was not pleased with no one' (DN, *NC)

(i.e., he was pleased with someone)

(Haegeman 1995:132)

---

[1] Postverbal negative subjects in Italian also require the negative particle *non*, as shown in (i).

(i)   *(**Non**) ha telefonato **nessuno**.

not   has telephoned no one

'No one has called.'

Finally, as the following examples show, the Russian NI-words, unlike Italian *nessuno* and French *personne*, do not occur in non-negative polarity environments (such as those that license English *anyone*).[2] For example, while the Italian negative constituent *nessuno* is licensed in Yes/No questions, as shown in (6a), Russian NI-words are not, as in (6b).

(6) a. Ha telefonato **nessuno**?

         has called   no one

         'Has anyone called?'

    b. ***Nikto** zvonil?

         no one called

The Russian question in (6b) is only grammatical with overt clausemate sentential negation indicated by *ne*, and then it only has the reading of a presumptively negative question: 'Did no one call?'.[3] The differences in the Russian NC pattern are summarized in (7).

(7) Russian NC pattern

    a. Negative pronouns in Russian can only occur when the preverbal negative clitic *ne* indicating sentential negation is present in the clause.

    b. Word order permutations do not induce a Double Negation reading.

    c. Russian NI-words do not occur in non-negative polarity environments.

3.2. The Status of Negative Constituents: Negative Polarity Items or Negative Quantifiers?

There has been a very interesting ongoing debate in the literature over the exact classification of negative constituents in languages that exhibit Negative Concord. The reason is that in some languages exhibiting NC, negative constituents often exhibit the behavior of both Negative Polarity Items (NPIs) and Negative Quantifiers (NQs), whose distinctive labels are motivated to account for the morphological and distributional distinctions between such English items as *anyone* (a NPI) and *no one* (a NQ) and to account for differences in their quantificational force and semantic behavior as well. In other words, some languages exhibiting NC use a single negative constituent as both an existential quantifier (NPI) on par with English *anyone* and as a universal quantifier (NQ) on par with English *no*

---

[2] Non-negative polarity environments include Yes/No questions, adversative predicates, and conditionals. I will return to this in Section 3.2.1

[3] I return to the role of negation in Yes/No questions in Chapter 5.

one. In the following sections I will outline these approaches and the burden of explanation associated with each.

3.2.1. The NPI approach (Ladusaw 1980, Linebarger 1981, 1987, Laka 1990, Progovac 1994)

The hallmark of Negative Polarity Items (NPIs) is that they require some triggering environment in order to occur. The canonical NPI licenser is clausemate negation for certain types of NPIs known as *strict* NPIs (e.g. the Russian NI-words), but certain NPIs can occur in other polarity environments as well, including **superordinate negation, Yes/No questions, conditionals**, and **adversative predicates** (i.e., predicates like *doubt* and *forget* that are assumed to be semantically negative).[4] English *any*-pronouns, which do not exhibit negative morphology or negative concord, are considered typical NPIs.

In some NC languages, negative constituents can also occur in these "non-strict" polarity environments and this has led the authors cited above to attempt to classify them as NPIs. For example, the Italian negative constituent *nessuno* ('no one/anyone'), in addition to occurring in NC clauses, can be interpreted as an existential and licensed by the Yes/No Operator, as was shown in (6a). Russian negative constituents do not follow this pattern. Russian negative constituents can occur only in the scope of clausemate negation, i.e., they behave like *strict* NPIs. They do not occur in any of the other polarity environments (cf. (6b)) .

The task for those who adopt this approach is to explain how negative constituents exhibiting NPI behavior in languages like Italian can also occur outside the traditional polarity environments and wield negative force independently, thereby behaving like negative quantifiers as we will see in the next section.

3.2.2. The NQ Approach (Zanuttini 1991, Rizzi 1982, Acquaviva 1992, 1993, Haegeman 1995)

The NQ approach treats negative constituents in NC languages as **negative quantifiers**, like English *nobody*, which are inherently negative and are interpreted universally. Unlike NPIs, NQs require no trigger. Instead they have independent negative force and can express negation without any other overt negative element present. Typical NQ behavior is seen in certain configurations with sentential negation, as shown in (8), or elliptically as an answer to a question, as in (9), both with an English *no*-NQ.

(8)   I have said **nothing**.

---

[4] Other examples of strict NPIs include English 'until' after non-durative verbs. Note the contrast between (i) and (ii):
(i)   Mary did**n't** leave **until** Steve called.
(ii) *Mary left **until** Steve called.
The pattern of strict NPIs differs from other NPIs, which can occur in polarity environments besides clausemate negation.

(9)   'Who did you see?' '**No one.**'

Compare (8) and (9) with the ungrammatical (10) and (11), which contain the NPI *anything*, but lack negation.

(10)   *I have said **anything**.

(11)   —Who did you see? —***Anyone**.

The English *any*-NPIs *anything* and *anyone* are not licensed in contexts lacking an overt marker of sentential negation (or some other polarity licenser), i.e., they cannot stand alone, as negative quantifiers can.

The arguments *for* negative constituents in NC languages being NQs and *against* them being NPIs are based on the fact that in certain contexts they behave like negative quantifiers. For example, Italian preverbal negative constituents occur without the marker of sentential negation and appear to suffice to negate the clause, as shown in (4) above. West Flemish negative constituents can also negate the clause on their own, as shown in (12) (example from Haegeman and Zanuttini 1996:

(12)   da Valère **niemand** kent

         that Valère nobody   knows

         'that Valère doesn't know anybody'

Russian negative pronouns also behave like NQs in that they can carry negative force on their own when used in elliptical expressions (13); however, they cannot in most instances be used in a full sentence without sentential negation (14).[5]

---

[5] I add the qualification "in most instances", since some prepositional phrases with the particle *ni* do seem to carry their own negative force, as in (i), from Kiklevič 1990.

(i)   On vernulsja **n i** s   **čem**.

      he returned   n o with what

      'He came back with nothing.'

Kiklevič gives two possible contexts for (i), one in which the person came back, but did not bring anything, and one in which the person did not come back and for that reason did not bring anything. This is shown again in (ii), also from Kiklevič 1990, and (iii).

(ii) On   postradal**n i** za **čto**.

      he   suffered n o for what

      'He suffered for nothing.'

(iii) On prišel bez   **ničego**.

      he came without no-what

      'He came with nothing.'

However, this appears limited to fixed expressions, as the ungrammaticality of (iv) without the negative marker *ne* shows.

(iv) On *(ne) byl tam   ni s   kem.

      he NEG was there n o with who

(13) Kogo ty videl? **Nikogo**.

who you saw no-who

'Who did you see?' 'No one.'

(14) Ja *(ne) videl **nikogo**.

I NEG saw no-who

'I saw no one.'

NQs can also be modified by certain adverbs, such as *almost* and *practically*, as shown in (15) for English *nothing*:

(15) Pat did (almost/practically) **nothing**.

Almost cannot modify NPIs like English *anything* as shown in (16a), but can modify negative constituents in NC languages, including the Russian NI-words, as in (16b).[6]

(16) a. *Pat didn't do almost/practically **anything**.

b. On počti **ničego** *(ne) delal.

he almost no-what NEG did

'He did almost nothing.'

The task before those who treat negative constituents as NQs is to explain why they can also occur in NPI environments where they do not yield negative force and are interpreted existentially.[7]

Determining the exact term with which to label the negative constituents in Russian is not the focus of this analysis. Rather I intend to provide a purely syntactic account of Negative Concord within the Minimalist framework that exploits the notion of morphology-driven feature checking developed in Chomsky 1995 and discussed in Chapter 2. I will show that the behavior and distribution of Russian negative constituents can be nicely accounted for by this approach. In addition, this analysis extends to the pattern of Negative Concord in other languages and provides a solid account, based on feature checking, of the variation in these patterns as well.

'He was there with no one.'

This phenomenon, of course, warrants further study. I intend to return to this in future work. For discussion of similar examples, see Billings 1995.

[6] This does not include generic or free-choice *any*, which does allow modification by *almost*, as in (i).

(i) Delmas will do *almost anything* (at all) to see a race.

This *any* is taken to be a universal quantifier. See Carson (19??) for discussion.

[7] For an interesting work devoted to capturing the mechanism behind the distinction between NPI and NQ interpretations of negative constituents in NC languages, see Giannakidou and Quer (1995).

3.3. The Structure of NegP in Russian

I assume (following Pollock (1989), Ouhalla (1991), and others), that sentential negation requires a Negative Phrase (NegP) as an independent functional category. What is the structure of this functional category in Russian? First of all, empirical evidence suggests that Russian requires the head of NegP to be overt, which I take to be the negative particle *ne* (following King (1993), Bailyn (1995a), Brown and Franks 1995, Brown (1995a, 1996a, 1996b). For example, as discussed above, sentential negation in Russian requires the negative particle *ne* as a proclitic on the verb (cf. Section 3.1). Furthermore, negative constituents (the NI-words) are not licensed without an overt negative head, namely the negative particle *ne*, as was shown in example (2).

In Brown and Franks 1995, we suggested that evidence of Relativized Minimality (RM) effects (cf. Rizzi 1990) indicate that the position [Spec, NegP] hosts a non-overt Negation Operator (Neg-Op). The proposed Neg-Op would block antecedent-government of the WH-trace in the embedded clause in (17) by the raised WH-adjunct *gde* ('where') causing the RM violation:[8]

(17) *?**Gde**$_i$ ty [$_{NegP}$ **Neg-Op** [$_{Neg}$**ne**]] skazal, čto Ivan ukral

     where$_i$ you   NEG said   that Ivan stole

     den'gi t$_i$?

     money t$_i$

     ?*'Where$_i$ didn't you say that Ivan stole the money t$_i$?'

In (17) *gde* can only be construed in the matrix clause, where the speaker is asking where the addressee did not make this particular statement and not about the location of Ivan's theft. In (18), on the other hand, which does not contain negation, and presumably there is no Neg-Op, the adjunct *gde* can colloquially be construed either in the matrix or the embedded clause.

(18) **Gde**$_i$ ty skazal, čto Ivan ukral den'gi t$_i$?

     where$_i$ you said   that Ivan stole money t$_i$

     'Where did you say (that) Ivan stole the money t$_i$?'

These RM effects supported our claim that the negated clause in (17) contains a non-overt Negative Operator in [Spec, NegP] that blocks antecedent-government of the trace of *gde* in the embedded clause by its antecedent in the [Spec, CP] of the matrix clause.[9]

---

[8] Note that I have modified the examples in Brown and Franks 1995 which were not actually RM violations at all.

[9] Note that only colloquial Russian allows adjunct extraction out of an embedded clause in any event. In the literary language this is not allowed. Note also that the complementizer *čto* 'that' is not optional, as it is in English.

Based on these claims, we therefore concluded that the structure of the NegP in Russian is as shown in (19):

(19)   Structure of Negation in Russian (from Brown and Franks 1995)

Since I am arguing that negation is expressed by an abstract [Interpretable] feature in the sublabel of Neg^0, I reject the structure where NegP has a Neg-Op in its Spec position. In order to assimilate that analysis I just assume that the abstract feature [NEG] overtly realized as *ne* constitutes the Negation Phrase and the abstract feature [NEG] replaces the Negative Operator, as shown in (20).

(20)   Structure of NegP

Under Minimalist assumptions, we need no Specifier position anyway. The Spec position will be "created" only if it necessary to host some overtly raised element that contains a feature relevant for checking in its sublabel, such as the feature [NEG]   on the NI-words. The Relativized Minimality effects associated with negation follow if we assume that Neg has both A and A' properties, a claim that finds empirical motivation in many languages (cf. Hornstein 1995 for further discussion).

3.4. Negative Concord and "Expressing Negation"

The task of the remaining sections is to show how this abstract [NEG] feature will account for the NC data in Russian, and by extension other languages. Recall from Chapter 2 (cf. especially Section 2.4) that movement in the Minimalist framework is economical and is morphology–driven by formal features. According to Checking Theory, inflectional elements move to have inflectional features checked in a Spec-head relation with an appropriate head marked with the same features. This is applicable, for instance, to NPs which move to have case features checked in the Specifier position of some functional category, the head of which is also marked with the appropriate case features. I will extend this analysis to negative constituents, which I treat as having negative features that must be checked and erased against the negative feature of the negative head.

Previous analyses of NC, most notably Haegeman (1992, 1995) and Haegeman and Zanuttini (1991, 1996), argue that the licensing of both WH-elements and negative constituents can be accounted for in accordance with the AFFECT-Criterion (21), which subsumes that WH-operators and NEG-operators are AFFECTIVE operators.

(21)   AFFECT-Criterion (Haegeman 1992)

a.   An AFFECTIVE operator must be in a Spec-head configuration with an AFFECTIVE] X⁰.

b.   An [AFFECTIVE] X° must be in a Spec-head configuration with an AFFECTIVE operator.

c.   AFFECTIVE OPERATOR: an AFFECTIVE-phrase in a scope position.

d.   Scope position: left-peripheral A'-position, i.e., an adjoined position [YP, XP] or a Specifier position [Spec, XP].

Both WH-elements and negative constituents are considered *affective* operators, and as affective operators they must be licensed in a Spec-head relation with an appropriate WH-head or NEG-head.[10]

The Spec-head configuration is schematized in (22), where [F] is the relevant AFFECTIVE feature.

(22)   Spec-head configuration

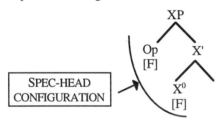

Under Checking Theory, the features [WH] and [NEG] would have to be checked against an appropriate [WH] or [NEG] head, respectively. Note, however, that this does not necessarily require that the feature on the head be checked as well. This feature simply enters into a Spec-head relation with the WH-element or negative constituent in order to satisfy the checking requirements of that element itself.

Recall from Chapter 2 that, according to Checking Theory, any **uninterpretable feature** must be checked and erased in order for a

---

[10] Note that not everyone considers these elements operators in every position. For example, Rizzi distinguishes between the **intrinsic** definition and the **functional** definition of operator. Those WH- and NEG-elements that are not configured as in (21d) are not operators, and therefore are not subject to the relevant instantiations of the AFFECT-criterion.

derivation to converge. Uninterpretable features include **Case Features** of the noun and **Φ-features** of the verb. Checking takes place in certain configurations allowed by Bare Phrase Structure, as shown in (5) in Chapter 2, repeated here as (23) (cf. Chomsky 1995).

(23)   Feature Checking

(a)   **Creation of a Specifier Position (Substitution)**: A YP (maximal projection) raises to create a checking configuration with an X^0 that has the appropriate feature in its feature sublabel (matrix). X^0 projects and a new projection XP = [YP X'] is created.

(b)   **Adjunction to XP** (a two-segment XP is created): A YP (maximal projection) raises to adjoin to a maximal projection (which can consist of a non-projecting head); a two-segment XP is created.

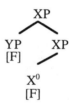

(c)   **Adjunction to X^0** (new zero-level maximal projection is created): A head Y^0 (or its non-overt feature sublabel) raises to adjoin to a head X^0; this is the only option for covert raising of features.

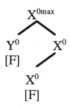

Notice the parallel between the Feature Checking configurations and the configuration for the NEG-Criterion in (22). As noted in Chapter 2, Bare Phrase Structure, does not require Spec positions, as (23b) and (23c) show. Within this framework, feature checking of [NEG] is morphologically driven. Importantly, checking the [NEG] feature does not necessarily entail both (21a) and (21b) of the NEG-Criterion. In other words, the [NEG] feature of the Neg head does not necessarily need to be checked.[11]

However, the [NEG] feature of negative constituents must be checked and erased in order for the sentence to receive a Negative Concord interpretation. This leaves only one feature expressing negation: the [NEG] feature of the negative head. In certain languages that exhibit Negative Concord, the negative constituents have a [–Interpretable] [NEG] feature that *must* be checked off and erased in order for the derivation containing them to converge; this accounts for the obligatory NC reading in those languages. These include Russian. In Russian the [NEG] feature in the sublabel of the NI-words is [–Interpretable] and must be checked against the head of NegP, which in Russian is always overtly manifested as *ne*; this checking is shown for (24a) by the partial structure given in (24b).

(24) a. Ja **nikogo ne**   videl.

       I no-what NEG   saw

       'I didn't see anything.'

    b. Checking [NEG] in Russian with overt raising of the *nikogo*

The feature [NEG] can also be abstracted from its host XP and move covertly for checking, forming the checking configuration in (23c) above. This allows the postverbal NI-word to remain *in situ* in (25a); checking of [NEG] with covert raising of the feature abstracted from a NI-word *in situ* is shown in (25b).

---

[11] Note that this is actually somewhat contrary to Minimalist assumptions about checking. There the feature that triggers movement for checking resides in the sublabel of the element that Attracts rather than on the element being Attracted. This is akin to Greed in earlier versions of the Minimalist Program, whereby an element moves to check its own feature. One possible way to circumvent this problem is having the [NEG] feature on Neg⁰ have some feature that must be checked by erasing all other similar features. It thus attracts the negative constituents and erases their negative features. This leaves the [NEG] feature on the negative head as the sole expressor of negation. This is in keeping with a recent analysis of WH-movement in Slavic by Bošković (to appear), which is developed somewhat by Brown (to appear), as well.

(25) a. Ja **ne** videl **nikogo**.

    I   NEG saw no-who

    'I didn't see anyone.'

  b. Checking of [NEG] with covert feature raising

As for multiple negative constituents that raise overtly or remain *in situ*, nothing in the Minimalist program prevents multiple Specs, so in these cases the [NEG] feature of the negative constituents would either raise to [Spec, Neg] to check itself against the [NEG] feature on Neg^0 and pied-pipe the negative constituent or remain *in situ* and only the [NEG] feature would raise. This is shown in (26).

(26) Checking of [NEG] on multiple negative constituents

  a. Ja **nikogo nigde ne** videl.

    I no-who no-where NEG saw

    'I didn't see anyone anywhere.'

  b. Partial structure of (26a)

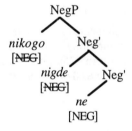

  c. Ja **ne** videl **nikogo nigde**.

    I NEG saw   no-who no-where

    'I didn't see anyone anywhere! (emphatic)'

  d. Partial structure of (26c)

3.4.1. NEG-absorption and the Interpretation of Multiple Negative Constituents: An Alternative Proposal

This analysis for Negative Concord in Russian handles one problem associated with analyses in terms of the NEG-Criterion, its dependence on the controversial Negative Absorption. In other words, within that framework, in order to ensure that multiple instances of negative words in a single clause express only one instance of negation once they have risen to satisfy the NEG-Criterion, they must undergo a process known as 'negative absorption' (cf. Higginbotham and May 1981, Zanuttini 1989, Haegeman and Zanuttini 1990, 1996), whereby the NEG-operators merge into one instance of negation by a process known as *factorization* as in (27):

(27) In languages that show NC, when two negative quantifiers raise they undergo a process which we will informally call "factorization": instead of creating two (or more) consecutive instances of a universal quantifier ($\forall$) each followed by an instance of negation ($\neg$), negation is factored out and the two (or more) universal quantifiers become one binary (or n-ary) quantifier:[12]

$$[\forall x \neg] \; [\forall y \neg] \; ([\forall z \neg]) \rightarrow [\forall x,y(,z)] \neg$$

(Ladusaw 1992: 242, citing Haegeman and Zanuttini 1990: 21-22)

This accounts for why multiple instances of negative words in NC languages do not give rise to a reading of Double Negation (DN) where each negative constituent is interpreted as independently negative. This is shown in the contrast between the Standard English example in (28), which exhibits DN, and the Russian example in (29), which exhibits NC.

(28) I did**n't** give **nothing** to **nobody**. (DN, *NC)

  (i.e. I gave something to somebody)

(29) Ja **nikomu ničego ne** davala. (NC, *DN)

  I no-who no-what NEG gave

  'I didn't give anything to anybody.'

The distinction between these two language types, as noted by Haegeman (1995), reduces to the fact that Standard English does not allow negative absorption, while a language like Russian does.

---

[12] Note that this is not the only possible interpretation of negative absorption. Ladusaw discusses several possible analyses of *factorization*, including one where negation ($\neg$) is factored out and takes scope over a merged existential quantifier ($\exists$), as in (i)

(i) $[\neg \exists x] \; [\neg \exists y] \; ([\neg \exists z]) = \neg[\exists x,y(,z)]$

See Ladusaw 1992 for further discussion.

Hornstein (1995) suggests that WH-absorption is superfluous and therefore incompatible with the Minimalist program.[13] Suppose we accept his claim and extend it to NEG-absorption. How might it be reinterpreted to account for the facts? Recall that, according to the literature, NEG-absorption must take place once the negative constituents have raised to [Spec, NegP] in order for the presence of multiple *n*-words in the sense of Laka 1990 to be construed as a single instance of negation (see also Haegeman and Zanuttini (1991) and Haegeman (1995)). Might we account for the distribution of negative pronouns observed in Russian (and all languages that exhibit Negative Concord, for that matter) without depending on absorption? Here I propose an account of the interpretation of multiple negative constituents that exploits the notions of feature deletion and traces as copies put forth by Chomsky (1995) and the notion of indefinites as variables developed by Heim (1988). This account in effect dispenses with the need for NEG-absorption.

As noted in Chapter 2, Chomsky suggests that once a given feature has been checked, it is deleted. This deletion canonically applies to inflectional and case features that are checked in a Spec-head relation with the head of an appropriate functional category. Reiterating the claim that the NEG-Criterion is reducible to Checking Theory, I propose that each negative constituent is semantically composed of a feature [NEG] taking scope over a non-specific indefinite whose semantic content is determined by the XP denotation of its WH-stem (cf. Table 1). In this respect, *nikto* ('no one') is semantically equivalent to [NOT an *x*, *x* a person] (or even NOT + 'who', its true morphological decomposition) as in (30) .[14]

(30) Semantic and Morphological Structure of Negative Constituents

a.	nikto	(ni + *who*)	'no one'	[NEG] [x a PERSON]
b.	ničto	(ni + *what*)	'nothing'	[NEG] [x a THING]
c.	nikogda	(ni + *when*)	'never'	[NEG] [x a TIME]
d.	nigde	(ni + *where*)	'nowhere'	[NEG] [x a PLACE]

What occurs in instances of multiple negation is that minimally the negative feature [NEG] of the negative constituent must be checked against

---

[13] The notion of absorption also causes problems for compositional semantics. See Ladusaw 1992 for discussion of these problems.

[14] This 'who' most likely will be a non-WH-element homonymous with a true WH-element, but actually synonymous with an indefinite. Empirical evidence supports the existence of such non-WH-homonyms, especially in those languages where WH-elements can behave as NPIs. Note the following example from Southern English:

(i) I don't know what about him. = 'I don't know anything about him.'

the [NEG] feature of the negative head in a checking relation, as in (23) above.

Either the entire negative constituent raises to check this feature or, in structures where the negative constituent occupies a postverbal position and presumably does not occupy [Spec, NegP] in the overt syntax, the abstract feature [NEG] covertly raises to adjoin to the head of NegP. Once checked, the [NEG] feature is deleted. Once the [NEG] feature has been deleted, the still present [NEG] feature in the sublabel of Neg^0 is interpreted as **negative closure** of events, i.e., sentential negation, and the negative pronouns are interpreted as indefinites in the domain of existential closure, i.e., the VP (cf. Diesing 1992).[15] This procedure is shown for (31a) in (31b).

(31) a. Ja **ne** vižu **ničego**.

        I NEG see   no-what

        'I don't see anything.'

    b. Ja $[_{\text{NegP0max}}$ [~~NEG~~] $[_{\text{Neg0}}$ ne [NEG] vižu$_i$ $[_{\text{TP}}$ t$_i$ **ničego**]]]

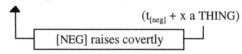

Here *ničego* ('no one') remains *in situ* at Spell-Out and the abstract feature [NEG] raises covertly to adjoin to Neg to be checked against the features of the head of NegP. Once the [NEG] feature is checked it is deleted. This leaves the WH-stem *in situ* representing the non-specific indefinite which, as a variable, is bound by existential closure VP internally (cf. Heim 1988, Diesing 1992); the post-deletion structure is shown in (32), where the [NEG] feature on Neg^0 induces negative closure of events.

(32) Ja $[_{\text{NEGP}}$ [**ne** [NEG] vižu$_i$ $[_{\text{TP}}$ t$_i$ [VP t$_i$ **čego**]]]]

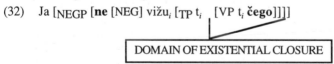

Assuming that verbs denote sets of events, the syntactic structure corresponds to the logical form in (33) in a formal language with events (cf. Parsons 1990).

(33) $\neg \exists e \in$ see : $\exists x$ thing $(x) \wedge$ Agent(e) = I $\wedge$ theme(e) = x

In other words, there is no event of seeing, such that there is a thing x and I see x.

In structures where the negative constituent has raised overtly, the entire negative constituent raises to [Spec, NegP] and leaves behind a copy in its

---

[15] The domain of existential closure is created by a process known as Tree Splitting, which will be discussed in great detail in Section 4.7.2.

base-generated position. Both copies at some pre-deletion point in the derivation consist of negation ([NEG]) + XP. The [NEG] feature of the lower copy deletes, since it is not required there for checking purposes. The higher [NEG] feature then checks itself against the [NEG] feature of Neg° and itself is deleted. The lower copy, as an indefinite, represents a variable bound by existential closure and the higher copy deletes. This can also be viewed as a type of post-Spellout reconstruction. The negative pronoun raises to have [NEG] checked in a Spec-head relation with the negative feature on Neg°, but the remaining indefinite is a variable that needs to be bound. Therefore the moved constituent is forced by LF interpretability to reconstruct to its base-generated position inside the VP and receive the proper existential interpretation, as in (34).[16]

(34)   Interpretation of Moved Negative Constituents.

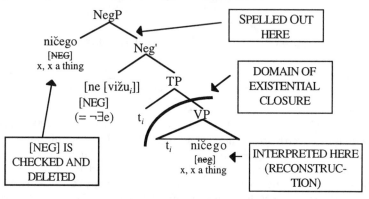

Similarly, multiple negative constituents (cf. (29)) raise overtly or remain *in situ*, as is shown in (31) and (34) for single negative constituents. Either way their [NEG] features are checked and deleted, and their copies *in situ* are interpreted as indefinites in the domain of existential closure. By making use of feature deletion and traces as copies, we dispense with the need for NEG-absorption. The feature [NEG] of the negative constituent is deleted for independent reasons, leaving no superfluous [NEG] features, while reconstruction back to its VP internal position allows the lower copy to be interpreted as an existential. The string of existential quantifiers in instances

---

[16] Note that the semantic breakdown of the NI-words parallels its etymological breakdown: *ne + i + k*-word, as seen in the historical development of the negative pronouns where the prefixes *ne* and *i* merged into *ni*. The prefix *i* occurs in other Slavic languages such as Serbian/Croatian, where it has an existential meaning in opaque contexts, as in (i):
(i)   Da li je Milan išta   doneo?
       C Q is Milan i-what brought
       Did Milan bring anything?'
Thanks to Wayles Browne for bringing this to my attention.

of multiple negative constituents can then merge into a polyadic quantifier, without the problems that beset NEG-absorption for compositional semantics (cf. Ladusaw 1992). Following the analysis developed so far, what actually expresses negation is the negative feature introduced in the sublabel of the negative head *ne*.

One particular advantage of the account proposed in this section is that it unifies the intuitions of NEG-absorption with the economical mechanism of feature deletion in the Minimalist program.[17] In addition, the analysis proposed here entails that it is the negative feature in the sublabel of Neg^0 with the semantics of negative closure of events that "expresses negation". This supports the claim by Ladusaw (1992: 328) that

> one does not associate a recognizable negation operator as the lexical interpretation of any of the visible formatives in the sentence, but rather with an abstract aspect of clause structure which must be licensed by a morphologically negative phrase.

Finally, it allows for both Spec-head feature checking and existential binding to be employed in the analysis of multiple negative constituents.

3.5. Parametric variation in NC patterns

Recall from Section 3.1 the various patterns of Negative Concord. There I outlined the basic differences between Slavic NC and other types of NC, including Italian. To review briefly, Slavic negative constituents, regardless of their configuration and how many of them occur, always require *ne*, the overt head of NegP, in order to be licit. This accounts for the ungrammaticality of (34a) and (34b) with no overt negative head:

(34) a. **Nikto** *(**ne**) zvonil.

 no-who NEG called

 'No one called.'

 b. **Nikto** *(**ne**) videl **nikogo**.

 no one NEG saw no-who

 'No one saw anyone.'

---

[17]A further advantage of this proposed analysis is that it parallels recent accounts of WH-raising in the literature (cf. Watanabe 1991). In these accounts the surface structure variations in WH-raising (multiple fronting in Slavic, fronting of only one wh-element, as in English, or no fronting, as in Chinese) result from parametric variation as to whether the WH-feature (or WH-operator as it is referred to in Watanabe 1991), can be abstracted from the WH-element, and if so, how many instances of this can occur. If we take the comparison between the account for WH-movement in Watanabe 1991 and the one proposed for NEG-movement (NEG-checking, NPI movement) in the current study one step further, we might suggest that in fact the [NEG] feature that is "abstracted" away from the negative pronoun is in fact an operator of sorts that must be checked.

In Italian, on the other hand, only postverbal negative constituents (either VP-internal or postposed) require the head of NegP to be overt. Preverbal negative constituents not only do not require an overt head of NegP to be present, they *cannot* cooccur with it. Thus *nessuno* ('nobody') in (35a) requires the presence of *non*, the head of NegP, because it is a postverbal subject. In (35b) *non* is required, because *nessuno* is a postverbal object.

(35) a. *(**Non**) ha   telefonato **nessuno**.

        NEG   has telephoned nobody

        'Nobody called.'

    b. Mario *(**non**) ha   telefonato **nessuno**.

        Mario NEG   has telephoned nobody

        'Mario didn't call anybody.'

The examples in (36) with a preverbal subject (36a) and a preposed constituent (36b) are ungrammatical with the negative particle *non* (from Haegeman 1995: 211, ex. (63a)).

(36) a. **Nessuno** (***non**) ha   telefonato.

        Nobody   NEG   has telephoned.

        'Nobody called.'

    b. A **nessuno** Gianni (%**non**) ha   parlato.[18]

        to nobody   Gianni NEG   has spoken

        'Gianni has spoken to no one.'

In addition, a negative subject licenses a postverbal negative constituent. The particle *non* is disallowed in these constructions, as in (37).

(37) **Nessuno** (***non**) ha parlato con   **nessuno**.

    nobody   NEG   has talked   with nobody

    'Nobody talked to anyone.'

This is also true of preposed negative constituents. The particle *non* is disallowed, as in (38) (compare with (36b)).

(38) A **nessuno** Gianni (***non**) dice **niente**.

    to no one   Gianni NEG   said nothing

    'Gianni does not say anything to anyone.'

This pattern also occurs in Spanish.

---

[18] The symbol % is used by Haegeman, as far as I can understand, to indicate that this example is grammatical with a slight focus on the preposed constituent.

In Standard English, unlike Italian and Russian-type languages, negative constituents do not exhibit patterns of Negative Concord. Only one negative constituent per sentence is allowed. Otherwise the reading is one of Double Negation. This is shown in (39a-c).

(39) a. **Nobody** ever went anywhere/***Nobody never** went **nowhere**.

b. **Nobody** came/***Nobody** didn't come.

c. I saw **nobody**/*I didn't see **nobody**.[19]

Catalan behaves like both Italian and Russian. Preverbal negative constituents can cooccur with the negative particle *no*, as the are required to do in Russian, but do not have to, as they are prohibited from doing in Italian. This is shown in (40) taken from Ladusaw (1992: 250, his (24f) and (24g)).

(40) a. **Ningú** (**no**) ha vist en Joan.

nobody NEG has seen DEF John

'No one has seen John.'

b. En Pere **mai** (**no**) fa **res**.

DEF Peter never NEG does nothing

'Peter never does anything.'

With postverbal negative constituents, on the other hand, the negative particle or a preverbal negative constituent is obligatory, as in (41), also from Ladusaw 1992.

(41) a. En Pere *(**no**) ha fet **res**.

DEF Peter NEG has done nothing

'Peter has done nothing.'

b.*(**No**) m' ha telefonat **ningú**.

NEG me has called nobody

'Nobody has called me.'

c. En Pere *(**no**) renta **mia** els plats.

DEF Peter NEG washes never DEF dishes

'Peter never washes the dishes.'

---

[19] Note, as Steve Franks points out (p.c.), that even in dialects of English that accept the ungrammatical variants in (39a) and (39c), the ungrammatical variant indicated in (39b) is still out. Instead this is expressed as in (i).
(i) Didn't nobody come.
      (intended to mean: Nobody came.)
This parallels the Italian data.

Interestingly enough, this same pattern is attested in Old Russian (OR) and Old Church Slavonic (OCS). The negative particle *ne* was optional in the case of preverbal negative constituents, but was obligatory (or at least always attested) with postverbal ones. This optionality is shown in example (42), where the NI-word occurs without the particle *ne*, and (43) where it occurs with it. All examples are taken from Křížková (1968: 24).

(42) a. **Nъ niktože** vъzloži na nь rǫku. (OCS)

     but no-who   placed   on   him hand

     'But no one laid a hand on him.'

    b. **Ničego** že   sja   bojatь běsi,   tokmo kresta. (OR)

     no-what EMP REFL fear   demons except cross

     'Demons fear nothing but the cross.'

(43) a. **Niktože ne**   najętъ   nasъ. (OCS)

     no-who   NEG   hired   us

     'Nobody hired us.'

    b. ...jako svoego **nikto** že   **ne**   xulitь.... (OR)

     ...that own   nobody EMP NEG   slander

     '...that no one slanders his own.'

The order NI-word–V is the only word order attested where a NI-word does not cooccur with the negative particle *ne*. Postverbal negative constituents are attested only with the negative particle *ne*, as in (44):

(44) a. az že   **ne**   sǫždǫ **nikomuže** (OCS)

     I EMP NEG   judge no-who

     'I don't judge anyone!'

    b. i   **ne**   idjaše s   nimi **niktože**... (OR)

     and NEG   went   with   them no-who

     '...and nobody went with them.'

West Flemish also exhibits Negative Concord, but only when the negative constituents are in a certain configuration at S-Structure. Recall example (5a), repeated here as (45), which shows that the negative constituent must occur in a Spec-head relation with the negative head at S-structure in order for the NC reading to obtain.

(45) da Valère **vanniemand nie** ketent   (en)-was

    that Valère of   no one   not contented   **en**-was

    'that Valère was not pleased with anyone' (*DN, NC)

Example (5b), repeated here as (46), shows that failure of the negative constituent to raise overtly results in a reading of Double Negation, where the negative constituents cancel each other out.

(46) da Valère **nie** ketent **van niemand** (en)-was

      that Valère not contented of no one **en**-was

      'that Valère was not pleased with no one' (DN, *NC)

      (i.e. he was pleased with someone)

To summarize:

(47) Russian (RU), Catalan (CA), Italian (IT), Spanish (SP), Old Russian (OR), Old Church Slavonic (OCS), and West Flemish (WF) exhibit Negative Concord; Standard English (SE) does not;

(48) For **postverbal** negative constituents, RU, CA, IT, SP, OR, and OCS require on overt Neg-head;:

(49) For **preverbal** negative constituents, only RU requires an overt Neg head; IT and Spanish disallow it; in CA, OCS, and OR it is optional.

(50) Only WF requires an overt Spec-head relation for a NC reading;

In (51) I outline what any analysis of NC must account for:

(51) a. The lack of Negative Concord in SE;

     b. The obligatory Spec-head pattern of Negative Concord in WF;

     c. The **historical development** of Negative Concord in RU;

     d. The apparent competing grammars of CA, OR, and OCS (cf. IT and RU) with respect to Negative Concord;

     e. The patterns of cooccurrence of sentential negation markers with negative constituents (summarized in the chart below):

Negative Concord and sentential negation markers

	Russian *ne*	Catalan *no/* OCS, OR *ne**	Italian *non*
w/preverbals	OBLIGATORY	OPTIONAL	DISALLOWED
w/postverbals	OBLIGATORY	OBLIGATORY (*as attested)	OBLIGATORY

3.5.1. Russian

In Russian (RU) the negative marker *ne* is a head and is therefore always overt. The uninterpretable feature [NEG] of a negative constituent must be checked against the [NEG] feature in the sublabel of the overt negative head, regardless of whether the feature raises covertly, as with postverbal negative constituents, or overtly, as with preverbal negative constituents. This explains why (52) is ungrammatical without *ne*.

(52) Ja **nikogo** *(**ne**) vižu.

     I NI-who NEG see

     'I don't see anyone.'

The absence of *ne* entails the absence of the feature [NEG]; the [NEG] feature of *nikogo* goes unchecked.

3.5.2. Italian

In order to account for Italian (and also Spanish), I claim that, like Russian, the [NEG] feature is uninterpretable in Italian and must be checked for the derivation to converge. However, the behavior of Italian postverbal and preverbal negative constituents suggests that perhaps the status of the negative marker in Italian is different from that of Russian.

Recall that Italian preverbal negative constituents cannot cooccur with the negative marker *non*. The reason, I argue, is that the negative head in Italian consists solely of an abstract negative feature that requires overt content in its Spec position, perhaps some uninterpretable feature that needs to be checked for clause typing (see fn. 23).[20] This approach assumes that the negative marker *non* in Italian is actually a Spec that adjoins to Neg^0 to satisfy the requirements of the non-overt negative head.[21] In the case of a negative clause containing no negative constituents, the negative marker *non* is obligatorily merged into that position to provide overt content for NegP, as shown for (53) by the partial structure in (54).

(53) **Non** ha visto Mario.

     not has seen Mario

     'He hasn't seen Mario.'

(54)

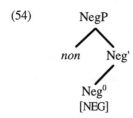

NegP

non   Neg'

Neg^0
[NEG]

---

[20] See Speas (1994, 1995) for claims that for a phrase to exist it must have either semantic or phonological content.

[21] Notice that this approach differs from that of Zanuttini (1994), who claims that the negative marker *non* in Italian is a head.

The particle *non* is not necessary in the case of preverbal negative constituents, since these overtly pass through [Spec, NegP] along with the feature [NEG], providing the overt content for NegP, as shown for (55) in (56).

(55) **Nessuno** ha   telefonato

  no one   has called

  'No one called'

(56) Movement of *nessuno* through [Spec, NegP] providing overt material

This also explains why postverbal negative constituents require the presence of the negative marker *non*. The sentential negation marker *non* is required, for the same reason it is required in a negated clause with no negative constituents present, i.e., because the negative head is non-overt and requires its Spec position to be filled. Since the feature [NEG] of a postverbal negative constituent raises covertly for checking and adjoins to the [NEG] which constitutes Neg^0, in clauses lacking *non*, a new zero-level maximal projection Neg^{0max} with no overt content would be created, as shown in (57).

(57) Neg^{0max} in Italian

The requirement that Neg^0 have an overt Spec is not satisfied and the derivation crashes. The negative particle *non* then is the necessary overt realization of Neg^{0max} and is required to merge as its Spec.

   Claiming that *non* is actually a Spec, together with the requirement that the Neg projection be overt also allows us to explain the pattern that occurs in Italian when postverbal and preverbal negative constituents cooccur as in (58).

(58) **Nessuno** (*non) ha   visto **niente**.

  no one   NEG has seen nothing

  'No one has seen anything.'

The particle *non* is necessary only to provide overt material for the Neg projection. In (55)-(56) and (58) this is provided by the trace/copy of the subject *nessuno* moving through [Spec, NegP] on its way to a higher position. The [NEG] feature of *niente* in (58) still raises covertly to head-adjoin to the [NEG] feature of the Neg head in order to be checked. However, nothing requires the presence of *non* to provide the overt material for that projection; this was done when *nessuno* passed through [Spec, Neg]. [22]

3.5.3. English

The analysis for Italian can be extended in part to Standard English. Here the negative head is non-overt, consisting only of the negative feature. The Neg projection requires overt phonological content and for this reason some overt negative constituent, either a *no*-pronoun (which might raise further for focus or Case checking) or the negative marker *n't/not* must be merged into the Spec position. This prevents negative sentences without an overt negative marker as in (59).

(59)   John called ≠ John didn't call.

Either a negative pronoun or adverb, such as *no one*, or the negative head *n't* can satisfy this requirement.

The difference between English and Italian lies in the fact that the [NEG] feature of *no*-pronouns in English is Interpretable and need not be checked. The only requirement that needs to be satisfied is the requirement that the non-overt Neg head have an overt specifier, satisfied by *n't* in (60) and *nobody* in (61) below.

(60)   John didn't see the movie.

(61)   Nobody saw the movie.

The cooccurrence in a clause of multiple negative constituents then results in a positive reading for the clause, since the negative features cancel each other out, as in (62).

(62)   John didn't see nobody. (DN)

Note that non-standard dialects of English which do exhibit Negative Concord would be analyzed exactly as Italian. These dialects disallow the cooccurrence of preverbal negative constituents with the negative particle *n't*, but require it for postverbal ones, as shown in (63)-(64) (my own examples). The contrast between (63a) and (63b) shows that preverbal negative constituents in this dialect do not cooccur with the negative marker

---

[22] As for the fact that Italian negative constituents can behave as NPIs and occur in non-strict polarity contexts (e.g., Yes/No questions, cf. (6) above), it may be that for Italian negative constituents any polarity feature can check off the [NEG] feature in their sublabel. In this way they behave similarly to NPs in Russian marked with Genitive of Negation in negated Yes/No questions, as will be discussed extensively in Chapter 5.

n't. While (63a) is fine, the pattern in (63c) is the preferred one for this utterance.

(63)   a.   Nobody has seen *Titanic*.

       b.   *Nobody ain't seen *Titanic*.

       c.   Ain't nobody seen *Titanic*.

       'Nobody has seen *Titanic*.'

The contrast between examples (64a) and (64b) shows that postverbal negative constituents require *n't*.

(64)   a.   *John saw nobody.

       b.   John ain't seen nobody.

       'John hasn't seen anybody.'

3.5.4. Old Church Slavonic, Old Russian, and Catalan

The data from these languages suggest that they have grammars competing between negation of the Italian-type and the RU-type; in other words the negative marker sometimes behaves like a Spec and sometimes like a head. This competition is visible only for **preverbal negative constituents**. When the negative marker is a head, as *ne* is in RU, it is always overt, and the negative feature of the preverbal negative constituents is checked by movement to/through [Spec, Neg]. When the negative marker is a Spec, as in Italian, then no negative marker is required for preverbal negative constituents since the negative constituent in Spec provides the overt content. Historically, we might propose, the requirement of a negative marker to provide overt material for Neg projections in sentences containing postverbal negative constituents in OCS and OR (and as seen in IT) led to a resolution of the competing grammars and the negative marker switched categories from a Spec to a head. Perhaps this is the destiny of Catalan.[23]

3.5.5. West Flemish

Checking of the [NEG] feature by overt movement is forced in West Flemish for a Negative Concord reading, because the feature [NEG] cannot be abstracted from its host XP (cf. Watanabe 1991 for a similar analysis of WH-movement parameters). The [NEG] feature of negative constituents in WF is Interpretable and can therefore go unchecked (hence unerased). This accounts for the Double Negation reading. All negative constituents in cases of non-movement retain their [NEG] features, which in turn cancel each other out.[24]

---

[23] Thanks to Steve Franks (p.c.), whose suggestion provided the framework for the analysis of cross-linguistic variation presented here.

[24] Of course the question arises as to what would force movement of the negative constituent to [Spec, NegP] at all in West Flemish if the [NEG] feature of the

3.6. Conclusion

In this chapter I have shown how a Minimalist approach involving feature checking can account for the pattern of negative constituents in Russian as well as the pattern observed in other languages, including Italian, Spanish, Catalan, Standard English, Southern English, Old Russian, Old Church Slavonic, and West Flemish. In the next chapter I continue in this spirit with an account of the Genitive of Negation in Russian negated clauses.

---

negative constituent is Interpretable. I can only suggest that perhaps what is taking place in West Flemish is that there is some feature on the Neg head that requires it to have an overt Specifier for clause typing as a negative clause. The failure of this feature to be checked, however, does not result in an ungrammatical clause in West Flemish, but rather one that is interpreted as positive, hence the Double Negation reading in those clauses. This is akin to a proposal by Chomsky (1997) that overt WH-raising occurs in those languages whose C has a [–Interpretable] feature that requires checking for clause typing. I leave this for future work.

Chapter 4: The Genitive of Negation

4.0. Introduction

In this chapter I develop a structural account of the phenomenon known as Genitive of Negation (GN). I first review its structural distribution and then discuss previous studies of GN. I then analyze the syntactic mechanisms that account for licensing GN. This discussion of GN together with the discussion in Chapter 3 on NI-words will provide the basis for the discussion of Expletive Negation in Chapter 5. These two chapters will also support the formulation of the status of negation within the phrase structure of Russian in Chapter 6.

4.1. Genitive of Negation: The Data

In determining the mechanisms for GN Case assignment, one must account for the wide range of data presented in examples (1) (8). First of all GN Case assignment is *optional* and depends on a wide variety of grammatical and pragmatic factors (cf. Timberlake 1975, Mustajoki 1985, Mustajoki and Heino 1991). Secondly, even if all the discourse conditions for GN Case assignment are satisfied, GN can still only occur on a *non-oblique VP-internal argument* of a negated verb. Therefore, GN (if assigned) is grammatical on the Obj of transitive verbs (1) and the Subj of unaccusative intransitive verbs (2), including existential verbs (3), since these are internal arguments. However, it is disallowed on the Subj of both transitive (4) and unergative intransitive verbs (5), as well as direct objects of verbs assigning some oblique case (e.g., Dat, Instr) (6).

(1) Internal Argument of Transitive

Ja **ne**   čitaju **žurnalov.**

I   NEG   read   magazines$_{GEN}$
'I don't read (any) magazines.'

(2) Internal Argument of Unaccusative

Otveta   **ne**   prišlo.

answer$_{GEN, MASC}$ NEG came$_{NEUT}$
'No answer came.'

(3) Internal Argument of Existential (from Babby 1980a) [1]

Moroza   **ne**   čuvstvovalos'.

frost$_{GEN, MASC}$ NEG felt$_{NEUT}$
'No frost was felt.'

(4) External Argument of Transitive

Studenty/*Studentov ne   čitajut/*čitaet   *Vojnu i mir.*

students$_{NOM}$/students$_{GEN}$ NEG read$_{3RD, PL}$/read$_{3RD,SG}$ *War and Peace*
'Students don't read *War and Peace.*'

(5) External Argument of Unergative

Studenty/*Studentov ne   spjat/*spit.

students$_{NOM}$/students$_{GEN}$ NEG sleep$_{3RD,PL}$/sleep$_{3RD,SG}$
'Students don't sleep.'

---

[1]Here I refer to verbs such as *čuvstvovat'sja* ('to be felt') as existentials, although Babby (1980a) makes the distinction between their use as existentials (asserting the existence of X) and declaratives (asserting an act of X). This distinction is made between (i) and (ii), where negation in (i) negates the performance by the elk of the act expressed by the verb *vodit'sja* ('to be/to live'), while in (ii) it negates the existence of the elk. Both are taken from Babby 1980a.

(i) Zdes' losi   ne vodjatsja.
 here elk$_{NOM,PL}$ NEG roam$_{3RD, PL}$
 'Elk don't roam here.'

(ii) Zdes' ne voditsja losej.
 here NEG roam$_{3RD,SG}$ elk$_{GEN}$
 'No elk roam here.'

(6) Oblique Direct Object

Vladimirov ne upravljaet **fabrikoj/*fabriki**.

Vladimirov NEG direct factory$_{INSTR}$/*factory$_{GEN}$

'Vladimirov doesn't direct the factory.'

Likewise, the derived Subj of negated passives (7) and themes in impersonal constructions with optional Dative experiencers (8, 9) can also occur in GN.

(7) Ne bylo polučeno **gazet**.

NEG was received$_{NEUT}$ newspapers$_{GEN,PL}$

'No newspapers were received.' (from Bailyn 1997)

(8) **Ol'gi** v zerkale vidno ne bylo, ne dorosla ešče.

Olga$_{GEN}$ in mirror visible NEG was NEG grow yet

'Olga wasn't visible in the mirror, she hadn't grown that tall yet.'

(from Aksenov 1994)

(9) Im ne nužno **sverkajuščix talantov**...

they$_{DAT}$ NEG need brilliant$_{GEN,PL}$ talents$_{GEN,PL}$

'They don't need any brilliant talents...'

(modified from Strugackij & Strugackij 1993)

Note that in each of the examples where GN occurs, it is optional; the argument marked GN can also receive either Nom or Acc Case. Therefore, in addition to accounting for the distributional restrictions on GN outlined in (1)-(8), we must also be able to account for its **optionality** as well as explain the Case that GN alternates with for each verb type. The nature of this Case alternation (GN~Nom or GN~Acc) depends crucially on the type of verb involved and, consequently, the grammatical role of the argument that exhibits the Case alternation. In structures with **transitive** verbs (10), for instance, GN always alternates with Acc, never Nom, on the **object**, while in those with **unaccusatives** (11), **existentials** (12), **passives** (13), and **impersonal predicates** (14)-(15), GN always alternates with Nom, never Acc, on the **subject**. The unergatives are irrelevant, since their arguments never display GN Case marking, i.e., there is no alternation with unergatives.

(10) Internal Argument of Transitive (cf. (1))

Ja **ne** čitaju **žurnaly**.

I NEG read magazines$_{ACC}$

'I don't read magazines.'

(11) Internal Argument of Unaccusative (cf. (2))

Otvet **ne** prišel.

answer$_{NOM, MASC}$ NEG came$_{MASC}$

'The answer didn't come.'

(12) Internal Argument of Existential (from Babby 1980a) (cf. (3))

Moroz **ne** čuvstvovalsja.

frost$_{NOM, MASC}$ NEG felt$_{MASC}$

'The frost wasn't felt.'

(13) Derived Subject of Passive (cf. (7))

Gazeta ne bylapolučena.

newspaper$_{NOM}$ NEG was received$_{FEM,SG}$

'The newspaper wasn't received.'

(14) Theme in Impersonal Construction (cf. (8))

Olga ne vidna.

Olga$_{NOM}$ NEG visible$_{FEM,SG}$

'Olga is not visible.'

(15) Theme in Impersonal Construction (cf. (9))

Takie talanty im ne nužny.

[such talents]$_{NOM}$ they$_{DAT}$ NEG needed$_{PL}$

'They don't need such talents.'

The relevant alternations are shown in (16).

(16) GN Alternations and Underlying Verb Structure

Verb Type	GN alternates with
1. transitive (accusative)	Acc
2. unaccusative/existential	Nom
3. unergative	—

In addition to determining the structural mechanisms that mark GN, the correct analysis must account for why, in a structure where GN can optionally occur, the GN-marked arguments tend to receive an **existential interpretation**, while those marked either Nom or Acc receive either an existential interpretation or a presuppositional/generic reading (as is shown to a certain degree in the glosses of (1)-(3), (7)-(9)). In fact, as discussed by Babby (1980a), the "Subj" in negated copular sentences with an existential reading is obligatorily in Gen, as in (17).[2]

---

[2]It is important to note that Nom *can* cooccur with a negated copula in sentences

(17) Knig/ *Knigi **ne** bylo na stole.

books_{GEN} books_{NOM} NEG was_{NEUT,SG} on table

'There weren't any books on the table.'

In the remainder of this chapter I develop a Minimalist account of the mechanisms of GN Case marking that will explain the facts discussed in this section, namely the distribution and optionality of GN, as well as the existential interpretation associated with it. First, however, I will briefly discuss previous accounts that have played a significant role in the development of my own analysis.

4.2. Previous Accounts of Genitive of Negation

4.2.1. Scope of Negation

As noted in Brown 1995a and Brown and Franks 1995, the study of the GN construction has probably given rise to a more copious body of linguistic research than any other single problem of Russian grammar. Corbett's (1986) bibliography of works on the subject is a dozen pages long, even though it only includes two publications more recent than 1979—Babby 1980a and Mustajoki 1985. While an exhaustive survey of this rich literature is the subject of a separate book, or even books, it is perhaps worth discussing some of the most important studies that focus on semantic and syntactic factors restricting the Genitive of Negation and on the mechanisms for its assignment.

Interestingly, all of the previous accounts of GN, regardless of whether they focus on the factors that condition GN or the rules that assign it, either explicitly claim or implicitly assume that GN can only occur on a Noun Phrase (NP) when that NP is in the scope of sentential negation.[3] For example, the direct object *knigi* ('books') in (18a) is Acc, because the sentence exhibits constituent negation (which is equal to being affirmative

---

such as (17) on the non-existential reading (i.e., the presuppositional or generic reading). In these cases, the subject is in Nom and the copula *byt'* ('to be') exhibits agreement, as in (i).

(i) Knigi/*Knig **n e** byli na stole.

books_{NOM}/books_{GEN} NEG were_{3RD,PL} on table

'(The) books weren't on the table (perhaps they were somewhere else).'

This distinction between locative and existential "BE-sentences" is presented and discussed extensively in Chvany 1975.

[3]In the remainder of the discussion I use the label NP (Noun Phrase), when referring to constituents such as the italicized ones in (i).

(i) *Studenty* ljubjat čitat' *interesnye knigi.*

students love to-read interesting books

'Students love to read interesting books.'

Note this corresponds to the Determiner Phrase (DP) in the discussion of Minimalism in Chapter 2. This in no way affects the analysis.

as far as GN assignment is concerned). However, the direct object *knig* ('books') in (18b) can be Gen, because *ne* expresses true sentential negation.

(18) a. Ja čitaju **ne** **knigi/** *knig, a **gazety**.

      I read NEG books$_{ACC}$ books$_{GEN}$ but newspapers$_{ACC}$

      'I am not reading books, but newspapers.'

    b. Ja **ne** čitaju **knig/** **knigi**.

      I NEG read books$_{GEN}$ books$_{ACC}$

      'I don't read books.'

Likewise the choice between Nom and Gen in negated existentials (cf. (3) and (12) above) is explained by differences in the scope of negation. For such sentences, Babby (1980a: 226) suggests that the Subj marked GN falls under the scope of negation and gives the sentence an existential reading, while the Subj marked Nom does not fall under the scope of negation and the sentence has a non-existential (i.e., declarative) reading (cf. fn. 1).[4]

4.2.2. The optionality of Genitive of Negation

Many accounts of GN focus on the fact that sentential negation is a necessary but not a sufficient condition for the application of the GN rule; the actual marking of genitive in examples comparable to (18b) is not obligatory, i.e., the argument *books* can also occur in Acc, as is shown. This is generally but not universally (cf. Bailyn 1997) taken to mean that in Russian GN Case marking is itself in some way optional. It is this optionality, and the search for factors alongside merely being in the scope of negation, that has been the focus of much earlier work on GN. The classic work on the optionality of GN is Timberlake 1975, which extends Jakobson's (1936) original insight that GN marks the quantification of (the lack of) participation in an event. In fact, the study of the various factors influencing GN dates back at least as far as Tomson 1903, which serves as a point of departure for the taxonomic study of factors influencing GN by Mustajoki (1985) and Mustajoki and Heino (1991). These works all to some degree or another focus on the communicative intent of the speaker and concentrate on how this influences Case selection for the direct object of a negated transitive verb.

4.2.3. GN is Distributionally Restricted

Actual mechanisms to formalize the rule that assigns GN have generally focused on the curious fact discussed above that—even if all relevant factors favoring GN are satisfied—only certain NP arguments are even eligible for GN marking (cf. Chvany 1975, Pesetsky 1982, Babby 1980a, 1980b, Neidle 1988, King 1993, Franks 1995, Brown 1995a, Brown and Franks 1995, Bailyn 1997). Let us review the two related instances where

---

[4] For Babby the logical subjects of existential verbs are actually the underlying subject.

arguments, although credibly within the scope of clausemate negation, can never undergo the GN rule.

First, subjects of transitives and unergative (but not unaccusative) intransitives, i.e., the VP-external arguments, cannot appear in GN (cf. (4)-(5)). These sorts of facts, discussed in Chvany (1975) and central to the theory of category selection put forward in Pesetsky (1982), would seem to require that the application of the GN rule be restricted to internal arguments of the VP, i.e., NP_2 in the structure in (19), thus apparently relinquishing any generalization about GN as a negative scope marker.

(19)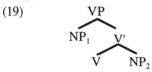

Therefore, in Government-Binding models, such as Pesetsky (1982) and Franks (1995), as well as Relational Grammar models, GN applies to underlying objects, while in Neidle's (1988) Lexical Functional Grammar analysis GN-marked subjects undergo a "demotion" rule to, in effect, become objects. Finally, for some linguists, such as Babby (1980a, 1980b), subject genitives do exist and can be characterized in terms of scope of negation (cf. Section 4.2.1).

Second, GN never applies to NPs that would be otherwise marked with some oblique Case; even among objects, only Acc NPs are candidates to receive GN under negation. This restriction is also discussed by the authors just mentioned, and is perhaps most prominent in the works of Babby, who invokes the dichotomy between configurational and lexical Case and imposes the condition that lexical Case is inviolate. Babby (1987: 95), for example, cites (20), in which a dative NP cannot be marked GN, even though it is clearly an internal argument in the scope of negation:

(20) Bogatye nikogda **ne** zavidujut **bednym/*bednyx**.

rich never NEG envy poor_{DAT}/*poor_{GEN}

'The rich never envy the poor.'

Although the direct object status of *bednym* may be debatable, there are other less controversial examples of oblique Obj NPs, such as the Instr Obj of the verb *upravljat'* ('to direct') in (6), that satisfy object tests such as passivization, as shown in (21) and discussed in Fowler (1996), but nonetheless fail to be marked GN:

(21) **Fabrika** upravljaetsja (Vladimirovym)

Factory_{NOM} is-managed_{REFL} (Vladimirov_{INST})

'The factory is managed (by Vladimirov)'

(modified from Franks and Dziwirek (1993, fn. 4))

These facts lead to the conclusion that GN not only just applies to internal argument NPs, but specifically to those that would not be marked for some oblique (or lexical) case.[5]

Provided, then, that there is some kind of tight structural restriction on GN, one might ask how it should be instantiated. While it seems correct that GN is only assigned to non-oblique NPs in direct object position, it is not obvious how that position should be defined. One might simply take it to be sister to V, as in much traditional work. Alternatively, following recent proposals by Bailyn (1995a, 1995b, 1997), one might posit a special position for GN case assignment. His basic Russian phrase structure is given in (22).

(22)   Russian phrase structure (Bailyn 1995a)

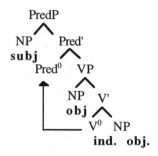

Following work by Larson (1988) and Bowers (1994), Bailyn (1995a, 1995b) posits three argument positions for Russian: the VP complement; the specifier of VP; and the specifier of PredP.[6] Since [Spec, VP], the highest NP position inside the VP, is the direct object position, this is where GN can be assigned. A process of Tree Splitting (from Diesing 1992) takes place, which marks VP as the domain of existential closure. The argument in [Spec, VP] at the time of Tree Splitting will be in the domain of existential closure and will receive Gen Case obligatorily. The asymmetries resulting from the lexical/configurational dichotomy in Babby 1987 now result from purely configurational distinctions among the various NP positions.[7] Finally, following recent proposals by Travis (1991), Chomsky and Lasnik (1993), Chomsky (1992), and Yadroff (1994), one might make use of the idea that structural (if not all) cases are checked in the specifier position of some independently motivated functional category, and

---

[5]We cannot simply conclude that Russian GN applies to NPs that would otherwise be accusative—as is indeed the appropriate characterization of the Polish situation—since unaccusative and passive objects, which would have no source for accusative case assignment, are also affected.

[6] Notice that PredP has been around as a constituent since Chomsky 1965.

[7]I will return to a more extensive discussion of Bailyn 1997 in Section 4.3.1.

assume that GN also operates in this way, as in Brown 1995 and Brown and Franks 1995a.

4.3. The Present Approach

In this chapter I develop a synthesis of the configurational VP-shell approach for Genitive of Negation of Bailyn 1997 and the functional category approach of Brown 1995a and Brown and Franks 1995. This analysis incorporates more recent developments within the Minimalist program regarding Checking Theory and phrase structure that account very nicely for Genitive of Negation, including its optionality, its structural limitations, and its semantic interpretation. This will require a more detailed discussion of Bailyn 1997, to which I devote Section 4.3.1. References to Brown 1995a and Brown and Franks 1995 will be made where relevant.

4.3.1. Bailyn 1997

Bailyn (1997) attempts a purely configurational approach to the assignment of Genitive of Negation whose main goal is, in effect, to eliminate the notion of optionality that has been a mainstay in the discussion of this phenomenon. Bailyn suggests that a given NP's occurrence in a unique configuration at the moment of existential closure will always result in that NP being marked GN (or **GenNeg** in his terms). In Bailyn's structure given in (23), the [Spec, VP] position is reserved for the so-called "direct object" that receives Acc or GN.

(23)   Russian phrase structure and Case marking (from Bailyn 1995a)

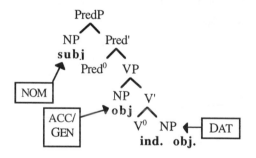

Bailyn presents support for this structure based on evidence from subject/object asymmetries and VP-internal argument asymmetries, such as reciprocal binding (24) and secondary predicate control (25).

    Bailyn argues that the binding facts for the reciprocal *drug druga* ('each other') in (24), where the Acc antecedent can bind the reciprocal in Dat, but not vice versa, naturally follow if the Acc argument c-commands the Dat argument. For this reason, (24a) and (24b), where the antecedent is in Acc and the reciprocal is in Dat, are fine, but (24c), where the antecedent is in Dat and the reciprocal is in Acc, is out; the Dat argument *Petrovym* does not c-command the Acc argument *drug druga* and therefore cannot bind it.

(24) *Reciprocal Binding* (from Bailyn 1995a)

    a. Mama predstavila **Petrovyx**$_i$ **drug drugu**$_i$.

        Mama introduced Petrovs$_{ACC}$ each other$_{DAT}$

        'Mama introduced the Petrovs to each other.'

    b. Mama predstavila **drug drugu**$_i$ **Petrovyx**$_i$.

        Mama introduced each other$_{DAT}$ Petrovs$_{ACC}$

        'Mama introduced the Petrovs to each other.'

    c. *Mama predstavila **drug druga**$_i$ **Petrovym**$_i$.

        Mama introduced each other$_{ACC}$ Petrovs$_{DAT}$

In order to get the appropriate binding facts for the secondary predicate structures in (25), Bailyn argues that Instr-marked secondary predicates are PredPs adjoined at the V'-level. With such a location, only the Subj or Obj can c-command these PredPs and therefore control their PRO subject, as shown in (26).

(25) *Secondary Predicate Control* (from Bailyn in press)

    a. Boris$_i$ našel **Sašu**$_k$ **golym**$_{i,k}$

        Boris found Sasha$_{ACC}$ nude$_{INSTR}$

        'Boris found Sasha nude.'

    b. Boris$_i$ sovetoval **Saše**$_k$ **golym**$_{i/*k}$

        Boris advised Sasha$_{DAT}$ nude$_{INSTR}$

        'Boris advised Sasha nude.'

(26) Structure of (25a) (= (14) from Bailyn (1995a))

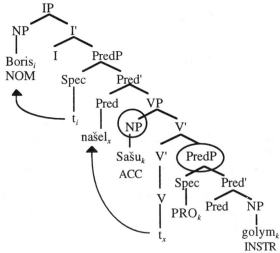

The Dat argument will be too low to c-command PRO, as shown in (27).[8]

(27)   Structure of (25b)

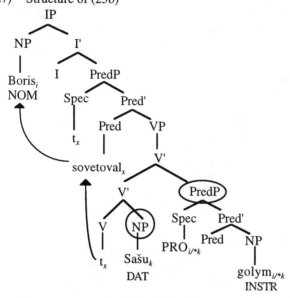

In order to account for GN within his framework, Bailyn proposes that NegP occurs in the structure in (23) as an "extended VP" just above VP, but below PredP. In this way, GN is assigned to the NP in [Spec, VP] via Exceptional Case Marking (ECM) by the Neg head, as in (28).

(28)   GN Case Assignment (Bailyn 1997).

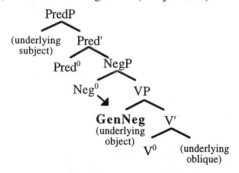

The relatively low position of Neg in the structure prevents it from governing and thereby assigning GN to the subject (i.e., external argument) position.

---

[8]Notice that this is the case only if we assume the first-branching node definition of c-command.

In order to obtain a distinct "Case-assignment" position for Acc, he designates [Spec, AgrO] as the checking position for this Case, following Chomsky 1993, as shown in (29).[9]

(29)   Case positions for Nom, Acc, & **GenNeg** (Bailyn 1997)

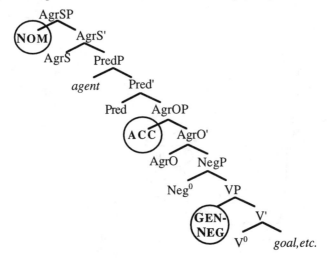

To explain GN Case assignment and checking, Bailyn adopts Tree Splitting (Diesing 1992, Diesing and Jelinek 1995) which divides the sentence into a **restrictor** and a **nuclear scope** at the VP, as in (30).

(30)   Tree Splitting (Diesing 1992)

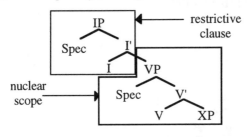

---

[9]Proposing such a fixed internal structure for all predicates does account for the data involving internal argument asymmetries that Bailyn discusses. However, as we shall see in Sections 3.5 and 3.6, this type of fixed structure runs contrary to Minimalist assumptions, which favor positing only structure that is necessary and do not entail such fixed internal argument positions. While I will maintain the VP-shell hypothesis proposed by Larson (1988) and adopted in various ways by Bowers (1994), Bailyn (1995a, 1995b, in press) and Chomsky (1995), I will propose an alternative to the fixed VP-internal configuration account for GN.

The nuclear scope (i.e., the VP) is the domain of existential closure; therefore, anything that remains in the VP when this splitting takes place will be bound by existential closure and receive an existential interpretation. What emerges outside the nuclear scope receives a generic or definite interpretation. Bailyn claims that GN Case marking is "obligatory on underlying (direct) objects still within VP when Tree Splitting occurs." For him Tree Splitting applies just above the NegP "as a kind of 'extended VP'". According to Bailyn, not only does this explain how GN is obligatory, but it also accounts for the existential interpretation that arguments marked GN receive. Bailyn suggests that Tree Splitting takes place at a separate level referred to as Functional Form (FF), and it is at this level that GN is checked, perhaps in [Spec, NegP].

Recognizing that Acc arguments, which in his analysis are checked outside the domain of existential closure in [Spec, AgrO], can also receive an existential interpretation in addition to a presupposed or definite interpretation, Bailyn adopts Diesing and Jelinek's (1995) proposal that either the head or the tail of a chain can be bound by existential closure. Therefore, despite the fact that the argument has risen to a position outside the VP where it is marked Acc, the tail of the chain created by that movement can still be interpreted in [Spec, VP], i.e., within the domain of existential closure. The notion that either the head or the tail of an argument chain can be interpreted (but not both simultaneously) is similar to proposals in Hornstein 1995 and Chomsky 1995.

While the fact that Acc arguments can receive an existential interpretation is accounted for, another problem remains. According to his configuration, even with the option to interpret either the head or the tail of an argument chain, the Subj will never be interpreted existentially, contrary to fact, without resorting to some process of LF lowering. This range of interpretations for the Subj can be seen in the different interpretations for the preverbal and postverbal subjects in (31) and (32), which Bailyn himself presents as an argument for Tree Splitting in Russian (his (27)). In (31) the preverbal subject receives a generic interpretation, while in (32) the postverbal subject receives an existential interpretation.[10]

(31) **Pticy** letajut.

      birds   fly

      'Birds fly.' (generic)

(32) Letajut **pticy**.

      fly   birds

      'Birds are flying.' (existential)

---

[10]These interpretations apply for these sentences with neutral falling intonation.

However, these examples cast doubt on the very structure for Tree Splitting in Russian that Bailyn is arguing for. Crucially the split in his analysis must occur just above the lower VP in the VP-shell structure (the higher VP being PredP in his nomenclature), in order to eliminate the Subj, which is base generated in [Spec, PredP], as a potential recipient of GN Case marking (cf. the structure for GN Case assignment in (29)). However, this also prevents *pticy* ('birds') from ever being in the domain of existential closure, without some sort of lowering operation to put it there. Neither the head nor the tail of the movement chain <*pticy, t (pticy)*> occurs within the domain of existential closure. In fact, Bailyn's analysis predicts that the Subj will *always* receive a generic or presuppositional interpretation. I return to this problem in Section 4.7.2, where I suggest that this can be accounted for if NegP marks the domain of "negative closure", and is above the outer VP shell rather than below it.

Bailyn (1997) puts the debate surrounding Genitive of Negation in a new and fresh perspective. In particular, the adoption of the Larsonian shell for Russian and Bowers' (1994) PredP structure will prove important in my own account of GN. However, certain problems need to be addressed, the most important being that his analysis will not account for the licensing of NI-words in Subj position. The Subj position will never be in the scope of negation, yet these pronouns do occur in Subj position, as shown in (33).

(33)   **Nikto ne**   zvonil.

no-who NEG   called

'No one called.'

Therefore, the account of why GN does not occur on (certain) subjects also incorrectly predicts that an NI-word can never occur in that position. The analysis of GN to be put forth in Section 4.6 will address this problem.

4.3.2. Brown 1995a and Brown and Franks 1995

In Brown 1995 and Brown and Franks 1995, following much recent work in Borer 1993 and Yadroff 1994 and stemming from Travis 1991, we adopt the idea that Cases are checked in the specifier positions of functional categories and extend this mechanism to GN as well. Our version of GN-Case checking is thus reduced to checking in a Spec-head configuration. We disregard the possibility of checking GN in [Spec, NegP] against Neg^0, given that we assume this to be an A'-position dedicated to a contentful covert Negative Operator accounting for sentential negation. We claim instead that GN is *checked* in the functional projection of the V^0 dedicated to checking object Case. Given that our proposed phrase structure, shown in (34), entails a close selectional relationship between Neg^0 and AspP, and because we assume (following Yadroff, among others) that Acc is checked in [Spec, AspP], we propose that GN also be checked in the Spec of the AspP complement of Neg^0.

(34)   Basic Negated Clause Structure ((12) in B&F 1995)

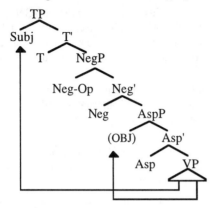

Initially we claim that the object raises to [Spec, AspP] as indicated in (34) and—when AspP is a complement to the head of NegP *ne*—this position can become associated with GN. This analysis is somewhat similar to that of Bailyn, except the position in our analysis is not one where GN is assigned by ECM, but rather one that is made a checking position for GN by virtue of its relationship with Asp. We eventually adopt Baker's (1988) Government Transparency Corollary (GTC), given in (35). According to the GTC the verb moves up the tree through each head position, picking up elements, such as Asp^0 and Neg^0 on its way up to T^0 or C^0 in Yes/No *li*-questions, as will be discussed in Chapter 5.

(35)   Government Transparency Corollary (Baker 1988: 64)

A lexical category which has an item incorporated into it governs everything which the incorporated item governed in its original structural position.

One necessary consequence of this movement is that Asp^0 incorporates into Neg^0, since Neg^0 is the immediately higher head, as seen in (34). By the GTC, this incorporation entails that Neg^0 now governs whatever Asp^0 does. Hence, the GTC provides a mechanism for the trace of Asp^0, having incorporated in Neg^0, to check GN through Spec-head agreement. Thus, the analysis in B&F depends on a selectional relationship between the head of NegP and its complement AspP, and stems from the requirement that V^0 raise at S-structure to pick up Asp^0, Neg^0, and T^0.[11]

---

[11] As a matter of fact, by adopting the GTC, we no longer really needed to make reference to any selectional relationship between Neg° and AspP, since by the GTC any functional category through which the V° moves will be able to check GN. In fact, this makes the prediction that any of the functional categories will be able to check the Case on a GN-marked argument.

4.4. What to account for

The present analysis captures the insights from the studies of GN discussed in Sections 4.2 and 4.3 within the Minimalist framework of Checking Theory and Bare Phrase Structure discussed in Chapter 2 in order to account for the following empirical observations associated with underlying verb structure and GN Case assignment:

(36) While GN alternates with Acc on the internal argument of negated transitive verbs (cf. (1) and (10)), GN alternates with Nom on the internal argument of negated unaccusative verbs ((2) and (11)) and existential verbs ((3) and (12)) .

(37) Case marking of the subject of negated copulas and unaccusatives (restricted to either Nom or Gen, *never* Acc) determines whether or not the sentence receives an existential interpretation.

(38) Acc and Gen never cooccur on internal arguments, assuming that all Case assignment is optional according to Minimalist assumptions, despite the fact that the inventory of functional categories allows for (at least) two distinct Case-marking positions for internal arguments.

(39) Subjects of transitives (4) and unergatives (5) can only be marked Nom, never Acc or Gen.

4.5. Case Marking, Case-checking Feature Complexes and the Internal VP Structure[12]

4.5.1. Case Marking and Case-checking Feature Complexes

Numerous proposals have accounted for the distinctive behavior of the different types of verbs by attributing to them a distinct underlying structure (cf. Larson 1988, Bowers 1994, Chomsky 1994, 1995, Hale and Keyser 1993a). I intend to show here with regard to Case marking that these distinct underlying VP structures, together with certain functional category features form Case checking feature complexes, ensure that the correct Case is marked on each argument and that nothing contradicts the empirical observations noted in (36)-(39) above. This account assumes that a single feature, or a combination of features created by head-adjunction of the verb to the head of a functional category, is responsible for the checking of a particular Case.[13]

Recall that Minimalist principles assume that the head H of a non-substantive category allows for the creation of a checking domain for a feature F on the head of a substantive category, if H contains F in its sublabel (i.e., feature matrix). The features of the original head H, as well as those of any heads that might have adjoined to H in the course of the

---

[12] The notion of feature complexes originates with Chomsky (1972)

[13] Which feature or features can actually create a checking domain for Case can in principle exhibit parametric variation.

derivation to give H^{0max}, constitute the sublabel of H whose features are visible for checking. Since the feature complexes that are relevant for our purposes are formed when the verb head-adjoins to a functional category, this amounts to having either the head of a functional category H_{FC} or a verbal head H_V that adjoins to H_{FC} contain the relevant features in its sublabel. The feature that needs checking (and whatever overt material is necessary for convergence) raises to form a checking domain and enter into a checking relation with the feature F on the sublabel of H (or H^{0max}). This checking relation is illustrated below in (40) for a maximal projection.

(40)   Checking Relation for Feature F on YP

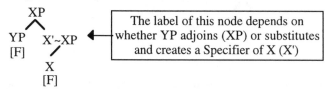

In this structure, YP raises to either adjoin to XP, creating a two-segment XP category, or to become the Spec of X. A checking relation can also be established between a head H_1 (or a feature of its sublabel) that adjoins to another head H_2, if H_2 contains in its sublabel an unchecked feature that matches some feature of H_1, as in (41).

(41)   Checking Relation for a Feature F via head-adjunction

In (41) H_1 raises to head-adjoin to H_2. Both processes illustrated in (40) and (41) create checking domains for the feature F.

While I do not exclude the possibility that the feature complexes that play a role in Case assignment may exhibit cross-linguistic variation with respect to which features account for which Case's checking domain, I will focus on those complexes that account for a wide variety of data in Russian. In view of the fact that the verbal head V in Russian, for reasons independent of Case, raises to head-adjoin to the heads of each of the appropriate functional categories (i.e., Tense, Aspect, Negation) to check certain features, I propose that the feature complexes involved in Case checking arise when some feature F_V intrinsically or structurally associated with V forms a complex feature sublabel via head-adjunction with some feature F_{FC} intrinsically associated with the head of the functional category, thereby creating a feature complex that will check and erase the matching Case feature on the appropriate NP.

To illustrate how this works, take the structure in (41). Let H_1 = the verbal head H_V and H_2 = the head of a functional category H_{FC}. H_V raises to head-adjoin to H_{FC} and the combination of FF_V and FF_{FC}, where FF_V and FF_{FC} are the feature sublabels of the V-head and the head of the functional category, create a new feature sublabel $FF_{FC}{}^{0max}$ of the complex functional head $H_{FC}{}^{0max}$. This feature label can check a particular Case, given the right combination of features. This is shown in (42).

(42)   Creation of $H_{FC}{}^{0max}$

The verbal features relevant to these Case-marking feature complexes are the structural features of the V determined by the type of verb [**±PRED**], [**±V^{max}**] (which, in a way to be made clear in Section 4.5.1, distinguish transitives, unergatives, and unaccusatives). The relevant functional category features are: (i) Tense (T) features ([**past**], [**present**], [**future**]); (ii) agreement, or Φ-features, ([**person**], [**number**], and [**gender**]), which occur on the head of T; (iii) Aspect (Asp) features ([**imperfective**], [**perfective**]); and (iv) Negation ([**NEG**]). The relevant feature complexes and the Cases they check are shown in Table (43).

(43)   Feature Complexes and Case Licensing

Feature Complexes	Case Licensed by Features
$[T, \Phi]$	Nom
$[Asp, +Pred, +V^{MAX}]$	Acc
$[Neg, +V^{max}]$[14]	Gen

---

[14]It turns out that the presence of a quirky case assigning feature [quirky case] blocks the creation of a checking domain for GN. This prevents the assignment of GN to internal arguments of verbs that assign quirky case, such as Instr, as in (6), repeated here as (i).

(i)   Vladimirov ne   upravljaet fabrikoj/   *fabriki.
      Vladimirov neg direct   factory$_{INSTR}$/ factory$_{GEN}$
      'Vladimirov doesn't direct the factory.'

Laurent Dekydtspotter (personal communication) points out that the PF manifestation of the argument *fabrikoj* in Instr may simply render the assignment of GN invisible on the surface. If this is the case then quirky case marking verbs also mark GN when negated. I leave this issue open.

In the next section I will show how these feature complexes account for Case marking for particular verb types and in Section 4.6 how they handle the facts for Genitive of Negation presented in Table (16) and in (36)-(39).

4.5.2. Underlying Verb Structure

In this section I outline the underlying verb structure adopted for each of the following verb types: (i) transitives; (ii) unaccusatives; and (iii) unergatives.[15] I also illustrate the involvement in Case marking of the feature complexes introduced in Table (43). This discussion will be assumed throughout the account of GN Case marking in Russian in Section 4.6, but can also be applied to Case marking in other languages. While I envision the Bare Phrase Structure outlined in Chapter 2, in many cases I still use the more familiar terminology associated with X-bar phrase structure for ease of exposition.

According to Minimalist assumptions about phrase structure, the verb V that is selected from the numeration (i.e., the list of components that will make up the final syntactic object if it converges) determines the θ-role assignment of its arguments, which is purely local. The underlying verb structure depends on the verb that is selected, and this verb determines not only the extent of its own internal structure, but the position and θ-role of its arguments.

As mentioned in the last section, the structure of the verb distinguishes **transitives**, those with both an external and internal argument, **unergatives**, those with only an external argument, and **unaccusatives**, those with only an internal argument. The complete VP structure being assumed is the PredP structure of Bowers 1994 and Bailyn 1995a given above in (23). The structure of each verb type within this framework is given in (44a-c).

(44)   a.   Underlying Structure for Transitive

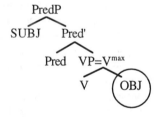

---

[15]Note that from here on I use the term unaccusative also to refer to the existentials illustrated in (3), (12), and (fn. 1), since their underlying structure is identical. Where important I will make the distinction.

b. Underlying Structure for Unergative

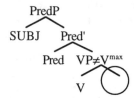

c. Underlying Structure of Unaccusative

The unaccusative will not even project a PredP shell, as in (44c).

From these structures we see that transitives are [+PRED], [+V^{max}], unergatives are [+PRED], [−V^{max}], while unaccusatives are [−PRED], [+V^{max}]. Since both transitives and unergatives have an external argument, these verbs can be distinguished by the feature [+PRED] from unaccusatives, which lack this VP-shell and are therefore marked [−PRED] . Transitives and unaccusatives, on the other hand, which both have internal arguments, i.e., VP = V^{max} = [V Obj], are distinguished by the feature [+V^{max}] from unergatives, which lack an internal argument and therefore have noncomplex VPs, i.e., VP ≠ V^{max} = [−V^{max}]. As we shall see below, these structural features together with certain functional category features will determine what type Case marking the arguments of a given verb type can display.

4.5.2.1. Transitive Verbs

Let us take a structure with a transitive verb to illustrate how the underlying verb structure depends on the verb that is selected, and how this determines not only the extent of the verb's internal structure, but also the position and θ-role of its arguments. Suppose a transitive verb V = *čitaet* ('read$_{3rd,sg}$') is chosen from the lexicon and also included in the numeration are two nouns: NP$_1$= *Sasha* and NP$_2$ = *gazeta* ('newspaper'). In creating the verb phrase, V determines the specific θ-roles of the various arguments (cf. Hale and Keyser 1993a and Chomsky 1995 for developments of this claim). In other words, the various structures that can potentially emerge in the creation of the VP and its shell determine the θ-role of the argument that is merged into that structure. Let us say that V selects NP$_1$=*Sasha* as the Subj (agent) and NP$_2$=*gazeta* as the Obj (patient). The configurational nature of θ-role assignment determines the underlying positions of these arguments, as shown in the structure in (45).[16]

---

[16]Notice that, in contrast to Bailyn's structure in (22), the structure posited here for a transitive verb without a complex internal domain places the Obj as the

(45)   Underlying Structure of a Transitive Verb

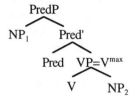

In the derivation, NP_1=*Sasha* is merged in [Spec, Pred] and in that configuration receives the agent θ-role by virtue of its relation to the term in the structure labeled Pred' = [Pred VP], while NP_2 = *gazeta* is merged as the complement to V and thus is assigned the patient θ-role. In a convergent derivation, the Subj=*Sasha* will receive Nom case and the Obj = *gazeta* will receive Acc, being realized phonetically as *gazetu*. Let us illustrate how this Case marking works.

Up to this point we have created the extended VP structure in (45) above. For simplicity's sake we will assume that the sentence will be an affirmative declarative of the form *Saša čitaet gazetu* ('Sasha$_{NOM}$ reads the newspaper$_{ACC}$'). Given this assumption, the next element to merge with the VP will be AspP, to which the V will eventually raise in order to check Asp features (and also possibly because Asp is marked [VERBAL AFFIX]). The transitive verb *čitaet* ('reads') intrinsically will be marked with the features [+PRED] and [+V^{max}]. Once V raises to head-adjoin to Asp, the newly created Asp^{0max} contains the features [+PRED], [+V^{max}], and [IMPERF] in its sublabel. This is illustrated in the structure in (46), abstracting away from other possible features.

(46)   Structure of Asp after head-adjunction of V_{TRANS} = *čitaet* ('reads')

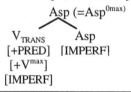

---

complement to the V, rather than the [Spec, VP] as Bailyn does, in effect relabeling VP = [Obj V'] as VP = [V Obj]. See Section 4.7, in particular discussion of (182) in Chomsky 1995 for motivation of this structure on principles of economy. In structures with complex internal domains, this structure would be identical to Bailyn's structure (cf. (23)). Note that the internal argument asymmetries that Bailyn uses this structure to explain will follow if we assume that binding relations are established at LF, and that Dat on the indirect object is some sort of configurational Case (still accepted, although not discussed in detail, in Chomsky 1995). Given this, the accusative argument will raise to be checked for Case, while the Dat argument will remain in its "base-generated" position. For this reason the Acc-marked argument at LF will always dominate the Dat-marked argument.

Notice that this Asp^{0max} contains in its sublabel all the features necessary to create a checking domain for Acc, according to the chart in (43). Since the only α marked Acc is *gazetu* located in the complement position to *čitaet*, by the definition of Attract/Move F in (47) (cf. (10), Section 2.6), the Obj *gazetu* is the only relevant α whose features are "attracted" by the combination of features on Asp^{0max}.

(47) K *attracts* F if F is the closest feature that can enter into a checking relation with a sublabel of K.

The Obj *gazetu* will then raise to create a [Spec, Asp] position and enter into a checking relation in order to have its features checked against the features in Asp^{0max}.[17] While the Nom Subj is closer to Asp, it is "invisible" for purposes of Acc Case marking, since it has no relevant features. Therefore *gazetu* raises by substitution to create [Spec, Asp], and the Acc Case feature of *gazetu* is checked and erased.[18] This is shown in (48).

(48) Acc Case checking

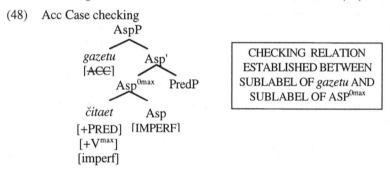

When T is merged, and the V moves onward to pick up its T features by head adjunction with T, the newly created T^{0max} contains the T feature [PRESENT], and the optional Φ-features [3RD PERSON] and [SINGULAR], which for verbs are –Interpretable and must be checked and erased. This combination of features creates a checking domain for Nom. Hence, the Φ-features in T^{0max} must also match those of the substantive category that moves into [Spec, T] to check Nom Case. This combination of features on

---

[17]For ease of exposition, I describe this process in the text as the Obj itself raising to create [Spec, Asp] in order to check its Case features. However, in many cases, it is not the Obj that overtly raises, but rather the feature sublabel FF_{obj} of the Obj that raises covertly and head-adjoins to Asp^{0max}.

[18]Note that [imperf] might also erase, if it is determined to be a –Interpretable feature. Recall that under Minimalist assumptions –Interpretable features are erased once checked, because they are invisible to the computation, and by the principle of Full Interpretation must be eliminated for convergence. It is most likely the case that this feature is either –Interpretable on the V or on Asp itself; in other words, one instance of this logically interpretable feature must be erased at LF.

T^{0max} attracts the only α marked Nom = *Sasha*, which raises to create a [Spec, T] position and enter into a checking relation with these features. Nominative Case is checked and that feature is erased from the sublabel of *Sasha*, as are the Φ-features in the sublabel of T^{0max}. This is shown below in (49).

(49)　　Nom Case Checking

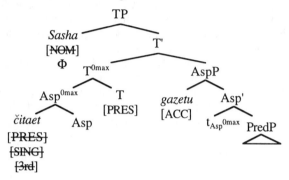

Assuming that all other necessary features are checked and eliminated, we have the following convergent derivation:[19]

(50)　Saša　　čitaet　　gazetu.

　　　Sasha$_{NOM}$　reads$_{3RD,SG}$ newspaper$_{ACC}$

　　　'Sasha reads the newspaper.'

If we follow the model in the text in which Merge and Move apply concurrently, the question arises as to why the Obj *gazetu* in [Spec, Asp] doesn't raise on to [Spec, T] to check the Φ-features on T^{0max}, since it is closer than the Subj *Sasha* in [Spec, Pred]. Under Minimalist assumptions there is no specification of which nouns have visible Φ-features, so the null hypothesis is that all nouns do, regardless of what Case they bear. However, the derivation in which the Obj *gazetu*, which has already had its Acc Case checked, raises to check the Φ-features in T^{0max} would crash because the Nom Case feature of the Subj *Sasha* would go unchecked. The Φ-features of the V will have been erased by the matching Φ-features of the Obj *gazetu* and along with them the checking domain for Nom Case. Since nothing prohibits raising of the Subj (the Obj is closer in terms of c-command, but not in terms of minimal domain) and only convergent derivations are

---

[19]In previous versions of this work (Brown 1996) it was assumed that Merge creates the structure at least to TP *before* Move occurs to check Case features. However, this was an erroneous assumption, because it conflicts with the nature of the Minimalist cycle, as pointed out to me by Željko Bošković (personal communication).

considered for economy conditions, the Subj will raise to [Spec, T] to check the Φ-features in T^{0max} and its own Nom Case.[20]

Now that we have illustrated the convergent derivation of a transitive structure, we must recall that, within the Minimalist program, the optionality, or randomness, of Case marking on a noun when selecting it from the numeration can result in the insertion into the derivation of a noun in the proper θ-position, but with improper Case marking. In order for the account just illustrated to be tenable, it must also be able to exclude incorrect derivations in the most economical way. Let us take a look at another transitive structure to see if this is the case.

Suppose we have chosen the same lexical items for the derivation as we did for (50) above. However, instead of optionally choosing the correct Cases for the Subj and Obj, we have marked the Subj with Acc (*Sashu*) and the Obj with Nom (*gazeta*).[21] This could hypothetically result in (51), which we know to be ungrammatical in Russian, given the θ-roles these arguments bear.

(51)   *Sašu   čitaet   gazeta.

Sasha$_{ACC}$ reads$_{3RD,SG}$ newspaper$_{NOM}$

to mean: Sasha reads the newspaper.

How does the present account prevent this derivation?

We begin with the structure in (52), which is identical in configuration to (45) above, except Subj is marked Acc, and Obj is marked Nom.

(52)   Transitive Verb Structure (with incorrect Case marking)

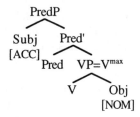

We proceed as before. First Asp Merges with the structure given in (52) and the complex [Pred-V] head raises to Asp to pick up its features. This creates a checking domain for Acc Case, as seen above. At this point, the NP

---

[20] Note that this is only an issue when the Φ-features of the Obj match those of the verb. Should they differ, we can assume that the Obj will never be attracted to check the Φ-features in T^{0max}.

[21] It is important to keep in mind that the θ-roles of the Subj and Obj are determined by their configuration and *not* by the Case they are marked with. Within the framework I assume here, θ-role and Case are independent of each other.

Sashu$_{ACC}$ in [Spec, PredP] is attracted by the feature complex, and it raises to [Spec, Asp] position. This is shown in (53).

(53)   Acc Case Checking

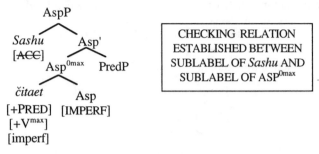

The next step of the derivation is the merge of, T. Asp^{0max} then raises to head-adjoin to T, creating a Nom Case checking domain, given the presence of T and the Φ-features in T^{0max}. At this point the Φ-features attract the closer NP with matching Φ-features *Sashu* in [Spec, Asp]. Since the Acc Case features of *Sashu* have already been checked, there is no feature mismatch. Nevertheless the derivation crashes, because the (illicit) Nom Case features on the Obj *gazeta* in VP go unchecked. Unlike the previous derivation, where the Subj marked Nom was able to raise over the Obj to check its Nom Case features when T merged, such movement cannot save this derivation. The Subj was able to raise there, because it was in the same minimal domain as the Obj and therefore equidistant from T, while in this derivation, *gazeta* in the complement position of V is not in the same minimal domain as the closer Obj and cannot raise over it to [Spec, T] to have its Nom Case features checked. The derivation is unsalvageable. This is shown in (54).

(54)   Nonconvergent Derivation of (51)

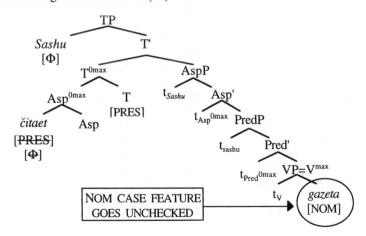

4.5.2.2. Unergative Verbs

In this section I turn to the internal structure of unergative verbs in Russian and show how Case marking for these verbs is limited to Nom Case on an external argument. Unergative verbs are those which by definition take no internal argument, hence do not assign an internal θ-role.

The VP structure that is created from unergative verbs, such as *spat'* ('to sleep'), is shown in (55).

(55)   Internal Structure of Unergative Verb

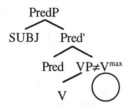

As discussed in Chomsky 1995 (cf. in particular pp. 315-316), the configuration [Pred VP] ([v VP] in his terms) expresses the agentive role and therefore obligatorily assigns that θ-role to the subject in [Spec, Pred]. For this reason failure of both transitives and unergatives, which project such a structure, to assign an external θ-role is interpreted as "simply meaningless". Note that unergatives have been referred to in the literature as "hidden transitives" (Hale and Keyser 1993a), which alludes to the fact that they, like the transitives, take an external argument and therefore project the outer VP shell, or PredP as in Bowers 1994, and assign it the proper θ-role associated with that configuration. Unergatives are marked with the projection features [+PRED] and [$-V^{max}$], since they have an external, but no internal argument.

Now that it has been shown how the relevant θ-role is assigned to the external argument of the unergative verb, it remains to show why that particular argument can legitimately receive no case other than Nom. As noted in the Table in (43), in order for a checking domain for Nom to be created, a combination of the tense feature T and the agreement Φ-features must be present in a given sublabel. This ensures that Nom Case only be assigned in [Spec, T] to a subject that agrees with the verb V that will eventually raise to T. The Φ-features on T^{0max} will attract the nearest NP in [Spec, Pred] to the [Spec, T] position. This is also a Nom Case checking position, given the presence of the Tense feature and the agreement Φ-features. Should any other Case-marked NP enter the derivation in the [Spec, Pred] position in the extended VP structure of an unergative verb, its raising to [Spec, T] will cause the derivation to crash due to feature mismatch.

How does this work? Suppose the verb *splju* ('sleep$_{1ST,SG}$') with the appropriate Φ-features optionally assigned is selected from the numeration along with the Subj *ja* ('I') which is inherently first-person singular. Suppose further that when *ja* is chosen from the numeration it is optionally assigned Nom Case. This gives us the VP structure in (56) after V raises to Pred.

(56)   Internal Structure of *splju* ('sleep$_{1ST,SG}$')

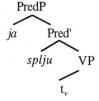

In the syntactic object created so far, the V = *splju* has the Φ-feature [1ST, SG] assigned optionally, but is marked [–V^{max}]. The derivation proceeds with each functional projection merging as above, and the verb raising to head-adjoin. Once the level of T has been reached in the derivation, the combination of the Tense feature [PRESENT], and the Φ-features [1ST PERSON] and [SINGULAR] will create a checking domain for Nom. Since the Subj *ja* is marked Nom, this NP raises, no feature mismatch occurs, this Nom Case feature is checked (as well as the Φ-features and Tense features of the verb), and the derivation converges.

What happens if the Subj of *splju* ('sleep') is optionally marked with Acc as it is entered into the derivation? Recall that a certain combination of relevant features are necessary for checking Acc Case, one of these being the feature F = [+V^{max}] associated with the verb that head-adjoins to Asp. In the case of the unergative verb *splju*, this feature has a minus value, therefore, no checking domain for Acc would ever be created to check the Case features on an Acc-marked Subj. The Subj will raise directly to [Spec, T] to check off the uninterpretable Φ-features on T^{0max}, but its Acc Case feature will cause a feature mismatch with its Nom Case checking feature sublabel, thus immediately canceling the derivation.[22] The proposal made here therefore prevents such ungrammatical structures as (57).

(57)   *Menja ne   splju/spit.[23]

         I$_{ACC}$ NEG   sleep$_{1ST,SG}$/sleep$_{3RD,SG}$

---

[22]Note that the issue of Acc not being checked does not even arise once a derivation has been canceled.

[23]I include the third person singular, which is taken to be the default form of a verb that has no subject to agree with, in order to show that the derivation does not crash because of Φ-features on the verb being unchecked, especially since intuitively *menja* ('me') is 1st person singular. Also relevant, perhaps, is the example in (i) below in the past tense, which has no person features, but does show gender—neuter being the default ending indicating lack of agreement with a subject. Even though no Φ-features need to be checked, the derivation will still crash because Acc Case on *menja* will go unchecked.

(i)   *Menja ne   spal/spalo.

         me$_{ACC}$ NEG   sleep$_{PAST,M}$/sleep$_{PAST,N}$

4.5.2.3. Unaccusatives

In this section I examine the internal structure and Case marking of unaccusatives. I will show that the account outlined so far will also handle the unaccusative data. The hallmark of unaccusatives is that they assign no external θ-role. Unaccusatives are thus marked [–PRED]. Their internal argument in affirmative constructions does not receive Acc Case, as is the case for internal arguments of transitives, but rather Nom. In a language like Russian with Case morphology, this is immediately apparent. Compare (58a) with the ungrammatical (58b):

(58) a. **Student** prišel.

 student$_{NOM}$ arrived$_{PAST,M}$

 'The student arrived.'

   b. ***Studenta** prišel/prišlo.

 student$_{ACC}$ arrived$_{PAST,M}$/arrived$_{PAST,N}$

Note, however, that the internal argument of the unaccusative verb *does* alternate with GN in negated clauses, like the internal argument of the transitive verb, as was shown above in (2) and repeated in (59). In such structures, the verb does not exhibit agreement with the internal argument:

(59) a. **Otvet** **ne** prišel.

 answer$_{NOM}$ NEG came$_{PAST,M}$

 'The answer didn't come.'

   b. **Otveta** **ne** prišlo.

 answer$_{GEN}$ NEG came$_{PAST,N}$

 'No answer came.'

In order for unaccusatives to avoid the θ-theory violations that arise for transitives and unergatives when the [Spec, Pred] does not contain a Subj, Chomsky (1995) suggests that within the Larsonian framework, the unaccusative verb creates only a simple VP, i.e., one with no shell. This conforms to Minimalist assumptions about phrase structure that only what is "needed" —in this case for θ-theoretic reasons— is projected. As pointed out by Steve Franks (p.c.), it also suggests a way to handle Burzio's generalization, which states that internal arguments of unaccusatives cannot receive Case. In a Bare Phrase Structure framework, it is Pred (or the light verb *v* in Chomsky's terms) in the extended VP shell that distinguishes between transitives and unaccusatives, i.e., the ability for the internal argument of the latter to receive Case other than Acc.[24] The following

---

[24]This can be seen in English by comparing the perfect with the passive. The participles are identical in these forms, but the auxiliary differs. This correlates with whether or not the internal argument of the participle is able to receive Acc Case, as in (i) and (ii) below.

structure adapted from Chomsky 1995 is henceforth adopted for unaccusatives.

(60)   Unaccusative Verb Structure

Let us now illustrate how in a simple declarative the unaccusative argument receives Nom Case, as in (58a). Suppose the verb *prišel* ('arrived$_{MASC,SG}$') is selected from the numeration and optionally assigned the appropriate Φ-features. This verb projects the structure pictured in (60). The NP chosen from the numeration enters the complement position and automatically receives the internal θ-role of the unaccusative verb. Keeping in mind that Case marking is random, we will mark the NP *student* with Nom. The resulting pre-raising VP structure is shown in (61).

(61)   Internal Structure of *prišel* ('arrived')

The structure reaches the TP level as before, and the features present in T^{0max} create a Nom checking domain. Since the internal argument of *prišel* is marked Nom, it raises to this checking domain, where its Nom Case feature is checked and erased.

Now suppose that when the NP *student* is picked from the numeration it is randomly assigned Acc rather than Nom and inserted into the complement position of V as *studenta* ('student$_{ACC}$'). How will we prevent this derivation from converging? Here we rely on the fact that unaccusatives are marked [–PRED], a feature which is required in order for an Acc checking domain to be created. In order to illustrate this let us pick the same verb *prišel*, except we will assign it no Φ-features so that it appears with the default neuter, singular ending as *prišlo* ('arrived$_{NEUT,SG}$').[25] The VP structure is shown in (62).

(i)   ... has eaten the cake.
(ii)   ...*was eaten the cake.
This follows if the transitive construction projects PredP, while the passive, identical in underlying structure to the unaccusative, does not even project this shell and therefore can never create an Acc Case checking domain.
[25]I do this in order to abstract away from the Φ-features that create a Nom case checking environment in T. This will show that failure to check Nom case is not the reason for the derivation to crash, nor is the failure to check the Φ-features of the verb; instead, the failure for the Acc Case feature on *studenta* to be checked and eliminated is the sole reason.

(62)   Internal Structure of *prišlo* ('arrived$_{NEUT,SG}$')

When Asp merges, V = *prišlo* raises to head-adjoin to Asp to pick up Asp features. This would be a checking domain for Acc, if the necessary combination of features were present. The sublabel of Asp^{0max} = [V – Asp] contains the Asp feature [PERFECTIVE] and the verbal feature [+V^{max}], but it is marked [–PRED]. Therefore no checking domain is created for Acc. T is then merged and the verb raises to T to pick up tense. This movement does not create a checking domain for Nom, because the necessary Φ-features are lacking. All features have been checked up to this point except the uninterpretable Acc Case feature on *studenta*, and there is no way for this Case to be checked, so the derivation crashes. [26]

4.5.2.4.   Conclusions

In the preceding subsections I put forth the claim that checking domains are created as a result of an appropriate combination of independently motivated features in a given head's feature sublabel, this combination being created for reasons independent of Case. I further showed how this proposal applies to transitives, unergatives, and unaccusatives, assuming a distinct underlying structure for each verb type.

   This theory of Case assignment has other welcome repercussions, which I will briefly mention here. Recall that in recent work (Yadroff 1994, Travis 1991, Chomsky 1995), there has been a drive to eliminate the Agreement (Agr) projections from the inventory of functional categories, since their sole purpose is to serve as Case-checking projections. Some linguists have proposed that the assignment of Case takes place in the Spec position of a particular functional category (Travis 1991, Chomsky and Lasnik 1993, Chomsky 1992, Yadroff 1994), while others (Chomsky 1995, Ch. 4) have suggested that VPs can allow multiple Spec-configurations that will account for the assignment of Accusative Case. While these proposals are aimed in the right direction, I believe there is room for improvement. Rather than stipulating that each Specifier of a functional category is uniquely associated with a particular Case (cf. Yadroff 1994 and Travis 1991), the proposal made here regarding checking domains for Case checking allows us to divorce Case assignment from the functional category *per se*. For example, we now no longer have to explain why in some sentences with Asp present Acc is assigned and in others it is not, which would be the case if a particular functional category is *always* associated with Acc. We would like variation in Case assignment properties to remain

---

[26] Should Φ-features be present, the unchecked Acc Case on *studenta* would cause a feature mismatch and the derivation would crash anyway.

in the lexicon. In this way, if all the relevant Case checking features (of which at least one, importantly, is contributed by the actual verb) are not present, no checking domain is created. Nevertheless, the independently motivated features on the functional head Asp, in the case of Acc Case marking, that can potentially contribute to the creation of this Case checking domain are checked anyway, presumably by features on the V-head, so that no uninterpretable features remain in the derivation at LF. The approach outlined here will be of particular importance in analyzing the mechanisms for Genitive of Negation, to which I now turn.

4.6. The Marking of Genitive of Negation

Based on the analysis of Case assignment presented in Section 4.5, it is now easy to see how to incorporate GN Case marking. Recall the facts in (63).

(63)   Facts of GN to account for:

    a.   GN can only occur on internal arguments;

    b.   GN is optional;

    c.   For transitive internal arguments, GN alternates with Acc;

    d.   For unaccusative internal arguments, GN alternates with Nom;

    e.   The NP marked GN tends to receive an existential interpretation, while the NP marked Acc receives a presuppositional or generic reading.

The explanations for the empirical facts in (63a), (63c), and (63d) can be explained in terms of the outline for Case marking and internal VP structure presented in Section 4.5. Given the phrase structure and the architecture of derivations that we are assuming, the fact noted in (63b) becomes irrelevant, since all Case marking of a NP drawn from the numeration is optional, i.e., random. The question we now turn to is exactly what allows an internal argument in a negated clause to alternate between GN and another Case, be it Acc or Nom, given that this sort of Case alternation, as is shown above, is blocked in affirmative clauses? Similarly, as we examine what effect this Case alternation has on the interpretation of the clause, we will discover the explanation for (63e).

4.6.1. Genitive of Negation and Feature Complexes

Before we account for GN Case marking and alternations with other Cases in negated clauses, it is necessary to add another independently motivated functional category to the inventory consisting of T and Asp that we have been working with so far in this chapter. This functional category is Negation, or Neg, which is introduced into the derivation in order to express negation. I showed in Chapter 3 how this category and its contents account for the licensing of the NI-words in Russian. In the following sections I will show how it accounts for GN.

Recall from Table (43) that the features that create a checking domain for GN are the negation feature [NEG] and the verbal feature [+V^{max}]. This allows GN to be marked on the internal argument of transitives and unaccusatives, but not on the external argument of unergatives (or transitives), since these are marked [–V^{max}]. Let us now see how this feature combination, together with the internal VP structure outlined above and economy principles subsumed in the Minimalist program, accounts for the interesting array of facts associated with GN.

4.6.2. Genitive of Negation and Transitive Constructions

In this section I discuss negative transitive constructions that parallel the affirmative constructions discussed in Section 4.5.2.1. I will demonstrate why this type of verb allows either a Gen or Acc internal argument, but does not allow either of these Cases on the external argument. In subsequent sections I will account for why the Nom~GN alternation is observed in unaccusative constructions, but not in transitive constructions.[27] This analysis must account for the empirical facts in (64), some of which were discussed in Section 4.5 with regard to affirmative constructions:

(64)   a.   The internal argument can be marked GN or Acc, but not Nom.

   Saša   ne   čitaet gazetu/   gazety.

   Sasha NEG   reads   newspaper$_{ACC}$ newspaper$_{GEN}$
   'Sasha doesn't read the newspaper.'

   b.   The internal argument cannot be marked Nom.

   Saša   ne   čitaet *gazeta.

   Sasha NEG   reads   newspaper$_{NOM}$

   c.   The external argument cannot be marked GN.

   *Saši   ne   čitaet gazetu/   gazety.

   Sasha$_{GEN}$ NEG   reads   newspaper$_{ACC}$/ newspaper$_{GEN}$

   d.   The external argument cannot be marked Acc.

   *Sašu   ne   čitaet gazetu/   gazety.

   Sasha$_{ACC}$ NEG   reads   newspaper$_{ACC}$/ newspaper$_{GEN}$

Let us choose from the numeration NP$_1$ = *Sasha*, NP$_2$ = *gazeta* ('newspaper') and V = *čitaet* ('reads'). Note that this numeration also contains [NEG] which is overtly realized as the negative particle *ne*. Say we insert *Sasha* (for θ-theoretic reasons) into the [Spec, Pred] position, where it assumes the role of Subj, and we insert *gazeta* into the complement to V position, where it becomes Obj. Suppose further that in our random Case marking as we

---

[27]Recall that the analysis of unaccusatives will also account for existentials and passives.

choose these lexical items from the numeration, we end up with *Sasha* as Nom, and *gazeta* as GN, giving *gazety*. This gives (65).

(65) Sasha   ne   čitaet gazety.

Sasha$_{NOM}$ NEG reads newspaper$_{GEN}$

'Sasha doesn't read the paper.'

How do we derive this structure? First we begin with the VP structure in (66) (=(45) with the Obj marked Gen).

(66) VP structure of *čitaet*

```
        PredP
        ╱╲
    Subj   Pred'
    [NOM]  ╱╲
        Pred   VP
              ╱╲
          čitaet  gazety
                  [GEN]
```

Here, instead of introducing Asp by the operation Merge right above VP, we merge Neg, which consists of (and therefore contains in its sublabel) an abstract feature [NEG], that expresses negative force. This places NegP below AspP for reasons regarding the existential interpretation of items that fall within the NegP domain, as will be discussed in Section 4.6.5. The feature [NEG] is overtly realized in Russian as the negation marker *ne*. I claim that that this feature is somewhat akin to the feature [Q] treated by Chomsky (1995: 289-297) as a formal feature of the Complementizer that indicates interrogative force of the clause. [NEG] is a formal feature of what is labeled the Negation phrase that indicates negative force.[28] Like [Q], [NEG] is Interpretable on the negative head, so in theory it does not need to be checked. However, this category does contain the feature [VERBAL AFFIX], since *ne* in Russian is a verbal proclitic. Hence, the V = *čitaet* first raises to head-adjoin to *ne* leaving traces in V and Pred, giving the structure in (67).

---

[28]In Chapter 5 I will discuss the possibility that this is not a Negation phrase, as has been traditionally labeled NegP, but rather a Polarity phrase (PolP) similar to that proposed in Laka 1990. This PolP can be marked with a feature [POL] that has a positive or negative value, the negative value [–POL] being functionally equivalent to [NEG] with all the relevant properties and indicating polarity reversal. I will return to this in Chapter 5 in connection with negated Yes/No questions. For now I stick to the more traditional terminology.

(67)   Structure of NegP

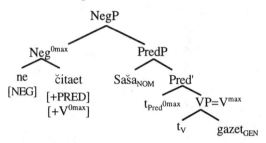

Notice that the sublabel of Neg^{0max}, once V has raised, contains the features [+PRED] [$+V^{max}$], and [NEG]. The presence of [$+V^{max}$] and [NEG] creates a checking domain for GN. Since the only visible α is the Gen–marked Obj *gazety*, the feature complex attracts the Obj, which raises to form [Spec, Neg] and have GN checked. The Gen feature of *gazety* is checked and erased as in (68).

(68)   Checking of GN

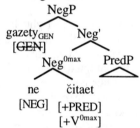

In the next step of the derivation the verb *čitaet* raises to head-adjoin to Asp, which has been merged above Neg, giving the structure in (69).

(69)   Structure of AspP

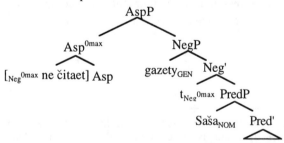

The newly created Asp^{0max} contains the Asp feature [IMPERFECTIVE], as well as the verbal features [+PRED] and [$+V^{max}$], which creates an Acc Case checking domain. However, there is no NP marked Acc to be attracted to this checking domain. Here the conclusions reached in the last section become relevant. Since the features that create the Acc checking domain are independently necessary and motivated, nothing happens if this checking domain is not utilized. The V then raises to head-adjoin to T, which has been merged with Asp. With the merging of T into the derivation a Nom Case checking domain is created. The NP *Sasha*, which is the closest Nom marked NP, raises to [Spec, T] to check its Nom Case feature and the Φ-feature in T^{0max}.[29]

Now that we have accounted for GN Case checking with transitive verbs, what happens if we optionally mark the Obj with Acc? Will the present proposal still account for this grammatical structure? The answer is yes. For simplification, I will skip the formation of the VP, assuming that is the same as that in (66) above, except in this case *gazety* is now marked Acc. Neg merges into the derivation and the verb raises to Neg, giving the structure in (70).

(70)   Structure of Neg

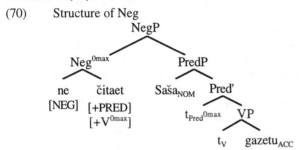

In this structure, as before, Neg^{0max} now contains in its sublabel the features that create a checking domain for GN. However, in this structure, there is no GN-marked argument whose case needs to be checked. Since the verb will have to raise onward anyway, this is ignored and the V raises further to head-adjoin to Asp. Once this takes place, the checking domain for GN disappears, given that traces are not visible as targets for checking (cf. Section 2.7). As above, an Acc checking domain is created due to the combination in the sublabel of Asp^{0max} of the appropriate features ([$+V^{max}$], [+PRED], and [ASP]). Since the Obj is marked Acc, it raises to create [Spec, Asp], thereby checking the Acc Case feature of the noun, which must be checked for convergence. T then merges as before, and a Nom Case checking domain is created; the Subj = *Saša* raises to create [Spec, T] and to check its own Nom Case and the Φ-features in T^{0max}. All uninterpretable features have been checked and the derivation converges.

What still remains is to show how the Case theory outlined above accounts for the ungrammatical Case marking in (64b-d) above, where the internal argument cannot be marked Nom, and the external argument can be

---

[29] The GN-marked NP *gazety* does not raise to check the Φ-features in T^{0max} for the same reason the Acc-marked NP did not raise in the derivation of (50).

marked neither Gen nor Acc. In Section 4.5.2.1 I accounted for this Case marking in structures lacking the Neg projection. Will the analysis also work for those containing Neg? Let us examine (64b) first, where the internal argument is marked Nom. For the sake of simplicity, I retain the same numeration: $NP_1 = Saša$, $NP_2 = gazeta$, V = čitaet, and [NEG] = ne. Suppose that the arguments receive the same θ-roles as in (65), except when selecting them from the numeration we mark both NP_1 and NP_2 with Nom Case, giving the incorrect structure in (71).

(71) *Saša   ne   čitaet gazeta.

   Sasha_NOM NEG   reads   newspaper_NOM

Since we know that the derivation in Russian of a structure with a transitive verb only creates one position for Nom checking (for the agent), i.e., [Spec T], we can immediately exclude this incorrect derivation, because one of the instances of Nom Case will go unchecked and cause the derivation to crash. Once the Φ-features have been checked and erased, the Nom Case checking domain no longer exists. Let us illustrate how this works. The verb raises through the functional projections as they merge as before. As it passes through Neg, it creates a GN Case checking domain; however, there is no GN marked argument, so it raises onward. It then creates an Acc checking domain in Asp, but there is no Acc marked. The merging of T, as before, creates a Nom Case checking position. The nearest NP marked Nom will be the NP *Sasha* in [Spec, PredP], which raises to check its Nom Case feature and the Φ-features in T^{0max}. T^{0max} no longer contains Φ-features, hence can no longer serve as a checking domain for Nom Case. The Nom Case on the Obj *gazeta* goes unchecked, thereby causing the derivation to crash. This is shown in (72).

(72) Nonconvergent Derivation of (64b=71)

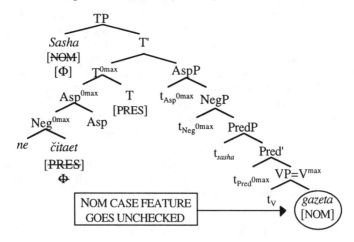

Suppose, however, that two Nom Case-marked NPs do not cooccur, but instead that the Obj *gazeta* is marked Nom, while the Subj *Saša* is marked GN. Will this analysis prevent such an illegitimate derivation? The answer again is yes. The closest NP with Φ-features, i.e., the GN marked Subj *Saši* will raise to check those features in T^{0max}, erasing the Nom Case checking domain for the Nom Case-marked Obj. The Nom Case-marked Obj is not visible to T, because it is not in the same domain, so it could not raise to T over the NP in [Spec, NegP]. It cannot attract its features covertly after raising of the GN-marked NP to [Spec, T], since the Nom Case checking domain has disappeared. [30]

4.6.3. Genitive of Negation and Unergative Constructions

In the last section I accounted for a wide range of data connected with GN and transitive constructions. I was able to account for why GN can only alternate with Acc on the internal argument of the transitive verb (cf. 64a-d). In this section I examine negated unergative constructions, in the hope of explaining why negated unergatives do not allow for any argument to be marked GN (or Acc, for that matter). What follows must be able to accommodate the empirical facts noted in (73), specifically, that there is no GN alternation on the external argument of these verbs.

(73) a. The external argument of a negated unergative verb is marked Nom.

Saša   ne   spit.

Sasha$_{NOM}$ NEG   sleeps

'Sasha doesn't sleep.'

    b. The external argument of a negated unergative verb cannot be marked GN.

*Saši   ne   spit.

Sasha$_{GEN}$ NEG   sleeps

    c. The external argument of a negated unergative verb cannot be marked Acc.

*Sašu   ne   spit.

Sasha$_{ACC}$ NEG   sleeps

This is easy to account for within the framework developed thus far. Recall that unergatives are marked with a negative value of the feature [V^{max}], which according to the theory being presented here requires a positive value

---

[30]As for the ungrammaticality of (64c-d), we will have to assume perhaps that Φ-features are only visible for NPs marked with Nom Case or those whose Case has not been checked, and the ungrammaticality of these examples is due to the [– Interpretable] Φ-features of T^{0max} not being erased, causing the derivation to crash. I will return to this issue below.

in order to create both Acc and GN checking domains. Should either Case occur on the external argument of an unergative verb, it will go unchecked and the derivation will crash, because it contains uninterpretable symbols and violates the principle of Full Interpretation.

4.6.4. Genitive of Negation and Unaccusative Constructions

Based on the arguments presented so far, I attempt in this section to account for the fact that the internal argument of negated unaccusatives and existentials alternates between GN and Nom, but not Acc. Contrast this with the fact that the internal argument of negated transitives alternates between GN and Acc, but not Nom. In other words, this proposal must be able to account for the following facts:

(74)   a.   The (internal) argument of a negated unaccusative can be Nom; verb agrees.

     Otvet   ne   prišel.

     answer$_{NOM}$ NEG came$_{3RD,SG,MASC}$

     'The answer didn't come.'

   b.   The (internal) argument of a negated unaccusative can be GN; verb does not agree.

     Otveta   ne   prišlo/*prišel.

     answer$_{GEN}$ NEG came$_{NEUT,SG}$/came$_{3RD,SG,MASC}$

     'No answer came.'

   c.   The (internal) argument of a negated unaccusative cannot be Acc, regardless of whether or not the verb agrees.

     *Sašu   ne   prišel/prišlo.

     Sasha$_{ACC}$ NEG   came$_{3RD,SG,MASC}$/came$_{3RD,SG,NEUT}$

Recall the structure of unaccusatives from (60) above, repeated here as (75):

(75)   Unaccusative Verb Structure

       $VP=V^{0max}$

       V   Obj

Suppose the numeration consists of the NP = *otvet* ('answer'), the V = *priš/l-* ('came'), and [NEG], overtly realized as *ne*. Given the structure in (75) for unaccusatives like *priš/l-*, the only position for *otvet* ('answer') is the internal argument position shown. Suppose that we mark *otvet* with Nom, and we assign the correct Φ-features [3RD PERSON], [SINGULAR], and [MASCULINE] to the verb. This gives us the structure in (76).

(76)   Structure of *prišel*

VP

prišel   otvet
[3RD]   ⌈NOM⌉
[SING]
⌈MASC⌉

The V raises through the various heads of the functional categories as they are merged, as outlined above. When Neg is merged, the V raises to Neg, and a GN Case checking domain is created. Since there is no GN-marked NP to have GN Case checked, Asp then merges and the V raises to Asp.[31] Because unaccusatives are marked [-PRED], no Acc checking domain is created at this step. A Nom Case checking domain emerges once T has merged and V raises to T. This attracts the internal argument *otvet* which is marked Nom. This argument raises to [Spec, T] and its Nom Case feature is checked and erased. The Φ-features in T^{0max} are also checked and erased. The derivation converges as (74a) above.

Suppose that instead of marking the Subj *otvet* ('answer') with Nom, we mark it with GN and assign no (or perhaps null) Φ-features to the verb, assuming also that T^{0max} does not carry these features either; this is realized as the default 3rd person, singular, neuter form, giving *prišlo* ('came'). After formation of the VP, we have the structure in (77).

(77)   Structure of *prišlo* with GN Internal Argument

VP

prišlo   otveta
[3RD]   ⌈GEN⌉
[SING]
[NEUT]

First Neg merges and V raises to head-adjoin to Neg. The new category Neg^{0max} contains in its sublabel the relevant features, i.e., the negation feature [NEG] and the verbal feature [+V^{max}], which together create a checking domain for GN. Since *otveta* ('answer') is marked GN, it is attracted to this checking domain to check these Case features. In this checking relation GN is erased from *otveta*. The verb raises further to check Asp and T features, but no new checking domain for Nom is created, since

---

[31]Note that a GN domain is created by the presence of the features [NEG] and [+V^{max}] , but there is no GN-marked α attracted to this domain. Just because a checking domain arises does not necessarily mean that it must be utilized, at least not in the case of GN, where the individual features that comprise the checking domain themselves need no independent checking.

neither the verb nor T have Φ-features. This derivation converges as (74b) with no verb agreement.

Here another question emerges: What happens if we do assign Φ-features to the verb? What prevents the derivation in (74b) (with verb agreement)? In this case, the Φ-features of the V and T will go unerased. Since raising of V to T will create a checking domain for Nom given the presence of Φ-features, no NP marked anything but Nom can raise to check off those features. However, there is no such NP present in the structure. This accounts for the ungrammaticality of (74b) with a GN-marked internal argument and verb agreement.

What remains to be explained is why the internal argument of these verbs cannot occur in the Acc. This goes back to the discussion above of affirmative unaccusatives and concerns the minus value of the feature [PRED] intrinsic in unaccusative verbs. Acc requires the feature [+PRED], so no Acc checking domain is ever created. For this reason any argument marked with Acc would be disallowed, since that [–Interpretable] Case feature would never be erased from the sublabel of the argument marked with it.

4.7. Genitive of Negation and the Existential Interpretation

Recall from Section 4.1 that one of the things that must be accounted for in any analysis of GN is the fact that arguments marked GN have an overwhelming tendency to receive an existential interpretation. This was analyzed by Bailyn (1995a, 1995b, 1997) as discussed in Section 4.3.1, and basically left on the back burner in Brown and Franks 1995. How might we account for this consistent observation given the present assumptions? At this point an analysis of negated copular structures proves to be quite revealing.

4.7.1. Negated Copulas

Copular structures in Russian have been the focus of several works, most notably that of Chvany (1975), who discusses the apparent divergent behavior of certain types of BE-sentences in Russian, i.e., those in which *byt'* (BE) is interpreted as an existential and those where it behaves simply as a grammatical copula marking tense and agreement. In her analysis the existential BE-sentences have two complementary interpretations, one where BE is synonymous with *naxodit'sja* ('to be located'), where the existence of the argument is presupposed, and one where BE is synonymous with *imet'sja* ('to exist, to be had') or *suščestvovat'* ('to exist'), which more or less asserts (or denies) the existence of the argument. Negated BE-sentences that receive an existential interpretation (where BE is parallel to EXIST), as in (78) from Chvany (1975:45), have been treated in the literature as always requiring a GN-marked Subj (cf. Babby 1980b, Bailyn (1997)).

(78)   V   gorode net **doktora.**

in   town   NEG doctor$_{GEN}$

'There is no doctor in town.'

Chvany claims that presupposed arguments in negated BE-sentences also occur in GN, as in (79a) (= (2.5b) from Chvany 1975: 47). For Chvany Nom-marked arguments of negated BE-sentences indicate the presence of an agentive variant of BE with an underlying Subj (external argument), not the existential BE, which has an underlying "direct object" (internal argument), as in (79b) (= (4.44a) from Chvany 1975: 157).

(79)   a. **Doktora** net v gorode.

          doktor$_{GEN}$ NEG in town

          'The doctor is not in town.'

    b. **Doktor**   ne   byl v gorode.

          doctor$_{NOM}$ NEG was in town

          'The doctor was not in town.' = 'The doctor did not go to town.'

The analysis presented here accounts readily for the structure of sentences comparable to those in (78)-(79). It also accounts for why (78) obligatorily receives an existential interpretation, while (79a) receives a presuppositional interpretation, despite the fact that this is existential BE and the argument is marked GN (contrary to claims made in Babby 1980 and Bailyn 1997). Likewise, it explains why (79b) cannot receive an existential interpretation. It does so without suggesting that BE has two distinct underlying structures, as Chvany does. It seems relevant that Case marking and verb agreement seem to be the determining factors in the interpretation of these structures, as has been previously advanced in earlier descriptions of these phenomena, which claimed that subjects of negated existential copulas are obligatorily GN. However, I suggest a slight reformulation of the interplay between syntactic form and semantic interpretation. Instead I claim that GN-marked subjects of negated copulas (as opposed to Nom) neutrally receive an existential interpretation (with certain word order). Given this, the analysis proposed here will accommodate these structures and their interpretation.

    To review, an analysis of negated copular structures must be able to account for the following facts:

(80)   a. Subjects of negated copulas *can* be Nom. These receive a presuppositional interpretation. Verb shows agreement. Order is neutrally SV(PP).

         Doktor   ne   byl/   *bylo   v   gorode

         doctor$_{NOM}$ NEG was$_{PAST,MASC,SG}$/was$_{PAST,NEUT,SG}$ in town

         'The doctor was not in town.'

b. Subjects of negated copulas can also be GN. Verb does not agree. These can receive an existential interpretation with neutral word order (PP)VS.

V gorode   ne   bylo/   *byl   doktora.

in town   NEG   was$_{PAST,NEUT,SG}$ was$_{PAST,MASC,SG}$ doctor$_{GEN}$

'There was no doctor in town.'

c. GN subjects of negated copulas can also receive a presuppositional interpretation. Word order is SV(PP).

Doktora   ne   bylo/   *byl   v gorode.

doctor$_{GEN}$ NEG   was$_{PAST,NEUT,SG}$ was$_{PAST,MASC,SG}$ in town

'The doctor was not (located) in town.'

d. Subjects of negated copulas receive no other case (i.e., Acc).

*Knigu   ne   bylo   na   stole.

book$_{ACC}$ NEG   was$_{PAST,NEUT,SG}$ on   table

Should the present account handle the facts dealing with negated copulas, it will be fairly straightforward to show that it will extend to other instances of GN that neutrally receive an existential interpretation.

I first examine the derivational processes that lead to the different Case-marking and verb agreement patterns above and then turn to how the various interpretations that result can be accounted for. Assume that BE in the structures above has the same internal structure as that of unaccusative verbs, as discussed earlier in this section, and is not marked with the feature [PRED]. In other words, the copula has a simple underlying VP structure, as shown in (81):

(81) Copular Verb Structure

In order to explain how the internal argument gets marked GN under nega-tion, we need only to recall that the proper feature combination for GN case assignment includes [NEG] and [+V^{max}]. Let us select an array of objects that includes [NEG], overtly realized as *ne*, the verb *byl-* ('was') and the NP *doktor* ('doctor'). These objects form the numeration. The verb *byl-* ('was') enters the derivation with no Φ-features, and is therefore realized overtly as *bylo* with the default neuter singular ending. We will randomly mark the argument as GN, so before the VP extends we have the following structure.

(82) Pre-Raising Verb Structure

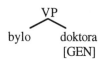

V raises to check its various functional features and to pick up the heads marked [VERBAL AFFIX]. V raises first to head-adjoin to Neg, creating Neg^{0max}. This zero-level maximal projection contains in its sublabel the necessary features for a GN checking domain, as in (83).

(83)   The GN Checking Domain

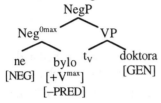

At this point the NP marked GN *doktora* ('doctor') will raise to this checking domain to check the GN feature in its own sublabel, and this feature will erase, as shown in (84).

(84)   Checking of GN on *doktora* ('doctor$_{GEN}$')

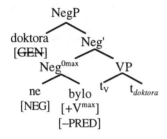

As the V raises further, no new checking domains are created, since the copula has the structure of an unaccusative verb and therefore lacks the feature [+PRED] (i.e., is marked [–PRED]) necessary for an Acc Case checking domain. There are no Φ-features to be checked or to create a Nom Case checking domain. All uninterpretable features have been eliminated and the derivation converges as (85).

(85)   V   gorode   ne   bylo   doktora.

        in   town   NEG   was$_{NEUT,SG}$ doctor$_{GEN}$

        'There was no doctor in town.'

I will return to why *doktora* ('doctor') is interpreted existentially momentarily.

    Another question arises: What would happen if upon entering the derivation from the numeration, the past tense verb optionally did receive Φ-features, and they matched the Φ-features of the argument, i.e., [3RD PERSON], [SINGULAR], and [MASCULINE]? How would we prevent this illegitimate derivation, shown in (86)?

(86)   *V   gorode   ne   byl   doktora.

        in   city   NEG   was$_{MASC,SG}$ doctor$_{GEN}$

Here the observation in fn. 30 becomes relevant again. It seems that nothing will prevent this derivation if the Φ-features of the GN-Case marked NP *doktora* are visible. I therefore adopt the postulate in (87) below in order to account for the relevant sentences ((64c), (64d), (86)).

(87)   Φ-Feature Visibility Postulate

   Once Case features of an NP have been checked, the Φ-Features become invisible for further syntactic operations, such as Attract.

The derivation of (86) will crash, because the only NP that could theoretically raise to check Φ-features is the GN-marked NP *doktora*, but this violates the Φ-feature Visibility Postulate.

   Now that the derivation of (85), with the argument is marked GN and no verb agreement, has been accounted for, let us return to (80a), where the argument is marked Nom and the verb does agree. The VP structure is as above in (82), except the NP *doktor* ('doctor') is marked Nom and the verb shows agreement. Let us pick up the derivation at the point where V head-adjoins to Neg, as in (83), creating the potential GN Checking domain in (88):

(88)   Potential GN Checking Domain

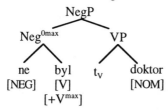

In this particular derivation there is no GN-marked NP. Since there is no GN-marked NP visible to this checking domain, the V raises further.[32] Once it reaches T, a Nom Case checking domain is created. The NP *doktor* raises to [Spec, T] checking its own Nom Case as well as the Φ-features in T^{0max}. The derivation converges. Note that an attempted derivation with a verb that did not have Φ-features would crash, because no Nom checking domain would ever be created and the Nom Case feature on *doktor* would go

---

[32]Recall that the checking domain does not necessarily have to be utilized during intermediate steps in the derivation if there is no visible NP with the appropriate features, given the fact that any uninterpretable features of V will be have to be checked and erased anyway. In this particular case, there are no features in the checking domain (i.e., the sublabel of Neg^{0max}) that need to be erased in the first place, so we lose nothing by not utilizing this checking domain. If a GN-marked NP had been present, these features would merely have collaborated to create a checking domain for the GN Case feature

unchecked. This prevents (89) with Nom Case on the subject and no verb agreement.

(89) *Doktor ne bylo v gorode.

doctor$_{NOM}$ NEG was$_{NEUT,SG}$ in town

Before turning to why and how word order affects the interpretation of these structures, let us see how this analysis prevents sentences in which the internal argument receives any Case other than Nom or GN (cf. (80d)). This should be fairly easy after the discussion of unaccusatives in Sections 4.5.2.3 and 4.6.4. Since I am assuming that unaccusative verbs are not marked with feature [PRED] at all, and the Acc checking domain requires the feature [+PRED], we see that no Acc checking domain will ever arise. This feature will go unchecked and the derivation will crash.

4.7.2. Tree Splitting and the Existential Reading

Up to this point the analysis has focused primarily on explaining the various possibilities for Case and agreement patterns that occur in structures that allow GN. I now turn to another important fact associated with the GN alternation, namely, that GN-marked arguments, be they Subj or Obj, receive an existential interpretation in neutral contexts, while arguments marked Nom or Acc (depending on VP structure) can receive either an existential interpretation or a presuppositional interpretation. This tendency has been observed and discussed for decades, as was noted in Section 4.3. Why might this be the case? I believe that the answer lies in the different locations of potential Case checking domains, as discussed extensively above and illustrated in (90).

(90) Potential Checking Domains (CH-DOMs) in the Tree Structure

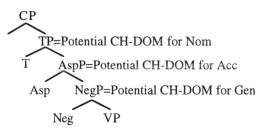

If we adopt for negated sentences the notion of "negative closure of events" suggested by Laurent Dekydtspotter (p.c.) (modified from Diesing's "existential closure" account as discussed in Section 4.3.1 and earlier in Section 3.4.1), whereby all elements interpreted in the c-command domain of NegP receive an existential interpretation, we can account for these observations. This differs from Bailyn's notion of NegP as a type of "extended VP" in that NegP occurs above the outer VP shell and takes the Subj in its scope.

I assume that arguments that raise for Case checking purposes form chains of the type $<\alpha, t(\alpha)>$, where α consists of either the overt argument or the non-overt feature sublabel of that argument. The element α forms the head of the chain. The trace $t(\alpha)$ of the raised element forms the tail of the chain in the base-generated position (the position where the argument receives its θ-role). Where do these argument chains fall in the structure with respect to negative closure, and might this have something to do with their interpretation? For GN-marked arguments we see in (91) that both the head and the tail of the chain of the argument marked GN fall within the domain of negative closure, the c-command domain of NegP.

(91) Domain of negative closure and the GN Chain

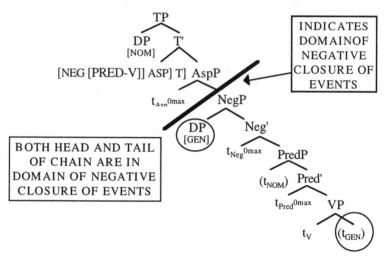

On the other hand, the heads of the chain of the Acc-marked argument and the Nom-marked argument fall outside this domain, while the tails fall within it, as shown in (92) and (93) respectively on the next page.

If we assume that an element can be interpreted at either the position of the head or the tail of the chain, we have a ready explanation. The GN-marked argument will always be interpreted within the domain of negative closure, while the arguments marked Acc or Nom can be interpreted either within that domain at the tail, and receive an existential interpretation, or outside that domain at the head, and be interpreted presuppositionally or generically. The fact that *doktora* in (79) receives a presuppositional interpretation and is simultaneously marked GN is related to its S_{GN}-V-PP word order, which is marked for existentials, the neutral word order for existentials of this type being PP-V-S_{GN}. In order for the GN-marked argument to receive this interpretation it has to move overtly so that it is interpreted outside the domain of negative closure.[33]

(92)   Domain of negative closure and the Acc Chain

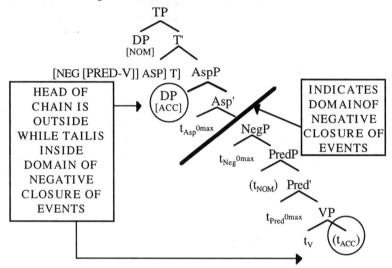

(93)   Domain of negative closure and the Nom Chain

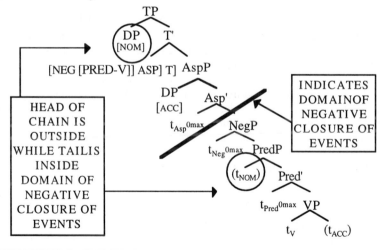

[33]Exactly where it moves to remains an open question at this point. The status of movement that is not driven by checking remains somewhat hazy within the Minimalist program. As Bailyn (1997) notes, this type of movement might take place in order to feed some functional level or Functional Form (FF) in his terms. It could be that this argument has a feature [+Topic] or [+Theme] that forces movement to a left-most Topic Phrase.

Notice that this explanation removes certain problems related to negative scope and the Subj position that accompany placing NegP too low in the tree structure, as Bailyn (1997) does (cf. Section 4.3.1). First of all, NegP now c-commands the Subj position, which will account for the fact that we get the negative NI-words in that position without resorting to some undesirable lowering operation, as in (33) repeated below as (94).

(94) **Nikto ne**   zvonil.

no-who NEG   called

'No one called.'

In this sentence, the NI-word can pass through [Spec, Neg] to check its [NEG] feature on the way to [Spec, T] to check Nom Case. Second, it accounts for the fact that the Subj can also receive an existential interpretation, which was an unnoticed contradiction in Bailyn's analysis. He argues for Tree Splitting on the basis of (31) and (32), repeated here as (95) and (96).

(95) Pticy letajut.

birds fly

'Birds fly.'   (generic/presuppositional)

(96) Letajut pticy.

fly   birds

'(Some) birds are flying.'   (existential interpretation)

In order for the subject *pticy* ('birds') to receive an existential interpretation in (96), it must be associated with the domain of existential closure. Given that the two links in this argument chain that are visible to the computation are located in [Spec, T] and [Spec, PredP] in Bailyn's configuration (cf. (22)), we assume that the tree for these affirmative statements is split into restrictor and nuclear scope just above PredP in order for the tail of the chain to be interpreted in the domain of existential closure. Given the surface word order, the feature Nom has most likely risen covertly to [Spec, T] for checking, leaving the overt argument in its "base-generated" position. This can also be seen in the contrast between (97) and (98).

(97) Deti   spjat zdes'.

children sleep here

'The children are sleeping/sleep here.'

(98) Zdes' spjat deti.

here sleep children

'There are children sleeping here.'

In (97), the external Nom-marked subject of the unergative verb *spjat* ('sleep') has raised to [Spec, TP] prior to Spell-Out and is interpreted outside the domain of existential closure. For this reason *deti* ('children') receives a presuppositional or generic reading. In (98) on the other hand, *deti* remains *in situ* and is interpreted in its base-generated position, i.e., the Spec of the outer VP-shell, or [Spec, PredP] in Bailyn's structure. I assume that the Nom feature has risen covertly to T for checking. Hence in (98) the Subj is interpreted existentially, suggesting that the domain of existential closure is in fact outside the outer VP-shell, rather than below it. However, in order to eliminate the external Subj as a potential recipient of GN in negated structures, Bailyn places NegP just above the internal VP and below PredP and designates the c-command domain of NegP as the domain of existential closure. However, with the domain of existential closure including only the lower VP, the Subj can never receive an existential interpretation. In order for the account that keeps external arguments outside the scope of negation to hold, there must be some sort of manipulation of how far the domain of existential closure extends, depending on whether the sentence is negated or not. With the present analysis, these problems are resolved: the external Subj of the unergative and transitive verbs will never be able to receive any Case other than Nom (cf. Section 4.5.2).

This section shows that the existential interpretation of GN-marked arguments in neutral contexts follows naturally from the fact that both the head and the tail of the chain of the argument marked GN fall within the domain of negative closure, which is induced at the NegP level above the bi-level VP-structure. The ability for Acc and Nom marked arguments to receive either an existential or a presuppositional interpretation also follows, since the tails of their argument chains fall within the domain of existential or negative closure, while the heads fall outside this domain. Depending on whether we interpret the head or the tail of these chains, the arguments receive either a presuppositional/generic or existential interpretation. The differences in interpretations of the various Case-marked arguments then reduces to the different positions of the Case checking domains in the derivation. From this it also seems possible to readjust the claim in Babby (1980b) and Bailyn (1997) that the subjects of negated existentials are obligatorily GN in favor of a claim that states that GN-marked subjects of negated copulas always receive an existential interpretation in neutral contexts.

4.8. Conclusion

In this chapter I developed a structural account of Genitive of Negation. I first reviewed its structural distribution and then discussed previous studies of GN then analyzed the syntactic mechanisms that account for licensing GN based on feature checking. This discussion of GN together with the discussion in Chapter 3 on NI-words will provide the basis for the discussion of Expletive Negation in the next chapter. These two chapters will also support the formulation of the status of negation within the phrase structure of Russian in Chapter 6.

Chapter 5: Expletive *ne* and the Asymmetry of Russian Negation

5.0. Expletive Negation: NI-words vs. Genitive of Negation

In this chapter I examine the behavior in Russian of pleonastic or expletive negation (cf. Brown 1995a and Brown and Franks 1995, 1997), which in canonical cases refers to negation that occurs in or is licensed by certain lexical expressions, but which itself is not semantically negative.[1] Such expressions include the subjunctive conjunction *kak by* after expressions of fear or worry as in (1), the phrase *čut' ne* ('almost') as in (2), and the phrase *poka ne* ('until') shown in (3).

(1) Ja bojus', **kak by**   on **ne**   opozdal.

    I   fear   how   MOD   he   NEG   was-late

    'I'm afraid he'll be late.'

---

[1] This phenomenon is familiar from Romance linguistics, but it also exists in the Slavic languages. See Grevisse (1988: 1492-97) for a discussion of expletive *ne* in French, as well as Espinal (1991, 1992) for expletive negation in Spanish and Catalan. For a discussion of West Flemish expletive *en*, see Haegeman (1995: 160-162).

94

(2)   On **čut' ne**   opozdal.

he   barely NEG   was-late

'He was almost late.'

(3)   Ja podoždu,   **poka** ty **ne**   prideš'.

I   will-wait   while you NEG   come

'I'll wait until you arrive.'

With regard to the expressions *čut' ne...* and *poka...ne*, Mustajoki and Heino (1991: 24) point out that it is "reasonable to treat *čut' ne* and its variants as examples of positive meaning in spite of the formal presence of negation," and refer to *poka...ne* as "another construction which can be said to have positive meaning in spite of its negative form (1991: 36)."

Canonical expletive negation exhibits very interesting behavior with respect to licensing NI-words and Genitive of Negation. Recall from Chapters 3 and 4 that NI-words and Genitive of Negation require clausemate negation bearing the feature [NEG] in order to be licit. In other words, they are licensed by clausemate (sentential) negation. However, as we see in examples (4)-(6), unlike true sentential negation, clausemate expletive negation in the fixed lexical expressions in (1)-(3) does not suffice to license the NI-words:

(4)   Ja bojus', kak by   **kto-nibud'/*nikto** ne   opozdal.

I fear   how MOD who-any/*no-who   NEG   was-late.

'I'm afraid someone will be late/*no one will be late.'

(5)   On čut'   ne   uronil   **kakoj-to/** ***nikakoj** stakan.

he barely NEG   dropped   which-some/ *no-which glass.

'He almost dropped some glass.'

(6)   Ja podoždu, poka   **kto-nibud'/** ***nikto**   ne   pridet.[2]

I   will-wait while   who-any/   *no-who NEG   come

'I'll wait until someone comes/*no one comes.'

---

[2] Tracy King (personal communication) points out that negation in expressions like *poka...ne* is not considered expletive negation by everyone. Piñon (1991) argues that negation in the corresponding construction in Hungarian contributes crucially to the semantics of the sentences that contain it. The definition of expletive negation in the text might then be modified to refer not to the semantics of negation *per se*, but to the syntactic force of negation with respect to certain phenomena that depend on it, namely the licensing of strict Negative Polarity Items, such as the NI-words. Expletive negation lacks this syntactic force. Nonetheless, it cannot be argued that negation in *poka...ne* does not negate the clause containing it, i.e., it does not reverse its truth value.

In examples such as these, either the indefinite *nibud'*-word or *to*-word is used, but never the negative NI-word.[3] At first we might simply dismiss this as irrelevant; the negative morpheme *ne* in these examples does not express negation; hence, the ungrammaticality of the NI-words, which require clausemate negation, follows in these contexts. However, upon closer examination we discover that this is not the whole picture. While what appears to be formally equivalent to sentential negation in these examples *cannot* license the NI-word, it *does* license Genitive of Negation, as we see in (7)-(8), taken from Brown and Franks 1995.

(7)   ...poka ne   poluču **vašego/ kakogo-nibud'/ *nikakogo**

       ...until NEG   receive [your/ which-any/   no-which

       otveta...

       answer]$_{GEN}$

       '...until I receive your/some/*no answer...'

(8)   Ja bojus', kak by   **kto-nibud'/ *nikto** ne   narušil

       I fear   how MOD who-any/   *no-who NEG   ruined

       èksperimenta.

       experiment$_{GEN}$

       'I'm afraid someone might ruin the experiment.'

An indicative perfective future clause introduced by the complementizer *čto* ('that'), as in (9) below, must otherwise be used to negate the embedded clause in (8):

(9)   Ja bojus', čto **nikto   ne**   narušit   **èksperimenta**.

       I   fear   that no-who NEG   will-ruin experiment$_{GEN}$

       'I'm afraid that no one will ruin the experiment.'

---

[3]Although the *nibud'-* and *to*-words normally do not occur in the scope of true clausemate negation, it is less interesting that the *nibud'-* and *to*-words can occur in these "negative" contexts than that the NI-words cannot. We find other examples of "attenuated" negation that allow the *nibud'*-words as well, as in (i), where negation is in the scope of a universal quantifier expressed abstractly by *kogda* ('when').

(i)   ...on xodit k bufetčice, kogda ona **ne** zanjata s   **kem-nibud'**
       ...he goes to waitress   when she NEG busy   with who-any
       drugim
       another
       '...he goes to the waitress's place, when(ever) she's not busy with someone else...'

This fact should be quite unsettling, since previous analyses of Genitive of Negation have linked its optional occurrence to whether or not the object NP marked with that Case occurs in the scope of negation (cf. Ch. 4). These data, however, demonstrate that GN occurs even when there is no negative force, and hence, no true scope of negation. The implicit assumption that sentential negation is necessary to license both NI-words and Genitive of Negation, despite their distributional differences, is apparently inadequate. Why might this be the case? What accounts for the pattern of expletive negation witnessed here, where NI-words are disallowed, but GN is fine? We shall see in this chapter.

5.1. Yes/No Questions and Expletive Negation.

5.1.1. Forced Expletive Negation and Yes/No *Li*-Questions

As it turns out, there is another purely grammatical environment in Russian that exhibits the same behavior observed with canonical expletive negation, namely negated Yes/No questions with the interrogative second-position clitic *li*. In negated *li*-questions the NI-words are disallowed, while GN is fine, as shown in (10).

(10) **Ne** dopustil **li** kto-nibud'/*nikto ošibki?

NEG allow Q who-any/ no-who mistake$_{GEN}$

'Could someone have made a mistake?'

It appears that the interaction of negation and interrogation when the [*ne* V] complex raises to C to host *li* is what forces this sort of behavior, hence the "forced expletive negation" analysis of Brown and Franks (1995). This pattern is also observed in non-*li* Yes/No questions with Subject-Verb Inversion where [*ne* V] has apparently raised to C. Why might negation be forced to be expletive in these cases? In Brown and Franks 1995 (see also Brown 1995a, 1996b) we claimed that certain independently motivated grammatical principles, including Rizzi's (1990) Relativized Minimality (RM), conspire to prevent negation from having negative force in specific syntactic environments, i.e., the *li*-questions, where the [*ne* V] complex raises to C to host the interrogative clitic *li*. In this chapter I offer a Minimalist reanalysis of this phenomenon that involves feature checking and mismatch.[4]

5.1.2. Optional Expletive Negation and non-*li* Yes/No questions

This reanalysis will also account for the fact that negated Yes/No questions without *li* and with no raising of the [*ne* V] complex to C can optionally exhibit this pattern. Note the following examples and their glosses:

---

[4] For an in depth discussion of Brown and Franks 1995 and the problems associated with that analysis, see Brown 1996b.

(11) A **kogo-nibud'** drugogo iz   podpol'ščikov ty **ne**   znaeš?

and who-any   other   of undergrounders you NEG   know

'So do you know anyone else from the underground?'

(12) A **nikogo** drugogo iz podpol'ščikov ty **ne**   znaeš?

and no-who other   of undergrounders you NEG   know

'So you know no one else from the underground?'

In (11) and (12) the [*ne* V] complex has not raised to C and either a NIBUD'-word or a NI-word is allowed.[5] Note that Genitive of Negation would be fine here in either instance.

5.2. Types of Russian Yes/No Questions

As modified from Restan (1969), Russian Yes/No questions fall into five main functional classes: (i) **purely informative questions**; (ii) **rhetorical questions**; (iii) **dubious questions**; (iv) **presumptive questions**; and (v) **emotionally-charged questions**.[6] The function of a Russian Yes/No question is closely tied in with its syntactic form, i.e., the word order of its constituents, whether it is negated, and whether it contains the interrogative particle *li*. Thus the occurrence of *li* and the pattern of expletive negation that occurs in negated questions, obligatorily when *li* is present and optionally when it is not, are closely connected with the formal and/or functional type of Yes/No question involved.[7] Therefore, before embarking on a syntactic analysis of expletive negation, in the

---

[5] Compare (11) to the negated declarative in (i), where the *nibud'*-word is disallowed:

(i) Ty nikogo/*kogo-nibud' drugogo iz   podpol'ščikov   ne znaeš.

You no-who/*who-any   other   of undergrounders   NEG know

'You don't know anyone else from the underground.'

[6] It must be noted that Restan's (1969) account of the syntax of interrogative sentences goes into specific detail about the statistical distribution in the different varieties of prose in his database of the various formal (vs. functional) classes of question, i.e., whether or not the constituents of such questions undergo Subject-Predicate inversion and whether or not the questions themselves contain the interrogative particle *li*. Restan concludes that the particle *li* occurs much more frequently in formal prose (*delovaja proza*) than in literary prose (*xudožestvennaja literatura*), given that the latter usually attempts to reproduce spoken dialogue, and *li* is falling out of use in the spoken language. The obligatory use of the particle *li* in contemporary spoken Russian is limited to embedded questions, while its optional usage in root clauses is encountered rather infrequently. Since I am not concerned here with stylistics, I do not focus on such tendencies in the discussion, but rather refer the reader to Restan's work.

[7] Despite the fact that it is falling out of use in root clauses in colloquial speech, wherever *li* is allowed in written Russian, it is also allowed (although not necessarily preferred) in spoken Russian.

subsections below I will briefly discuss the formal and functional classes of Russian Yes/No questions with respect to their allowance of the particle *li* and the occurrence of this pattern. This discussion, based on work by Restan (1969), will provide the backdrop for the analysis of expletive negation in interrogatives to follow in Section 5.4, where I demonstrate how by means of this pattern Russian actually provides overt syntactic manifestation of the pragmatic interaction between negation and interrogation.

5.2.1. Purely informative Yes/No questions

The sole purpose of a purely informative Yes/No question is to obtain information. Unlike the remaining categories, no pragmatic strategies play a role in this type of question; they are presuppositionally neutral. No particular reply is anticipated; a positive or negative answer is equally possible. In these questions the presence of formal negation does not carry negative implicature. As noted by Restan (1969: 298), negation as a sentential force in purely informative questions is neutralized:

> ...the negative meaning of the particle *ne* is somehow erased....For this reason *a purely-informative negative question is equivalent to the corresponding affirmative question*. The neutralization of the affirmative and negative forms, therefore, is a general characteristic of the purely-informative question [*emphasis and translation mine*].

The particle *li* frequently occurs and negated purely informative Yes/No questions with *li*, as expected, exhibit the pattern of expletive negation, as in (13).

(13) **Ne** uznal **li** ty čego-nibud' interesnogo v Peterburge?

NEG found-out Q you what-any$_{GEN}$ interesting$_{GEN}$ in Petersburg

'Did you find anything interesting out in Petersburg or not?'

(14) Gde Borja? Ty **ne** videl Borju?

where Borja you NEG saw Borja

'Where's Borja? Have you seen Borja?'

(15) Vy spite?

you sleep

'Are you asleep?'

(16) Veriš' ty mne?

believe you me

'Do you believe me?'

(17) Končilas' li vojna?

finished Q war

'Is the war over?'

Purely informative Yes/No questions can take a variety of forms, as shown in (13)–(17). In (13) we see the form [NEG–V–*li*–Subj]; in (14) the word order is [Subj–NEG–V]; in (15) we find [Subj–V]; example (16) takes the form [V–Subj]; and in (17) we see [V–*li*–Subj]. However, Restan (1969: 220) notes that inversion in non-*li* questions, as in (16), obligatorily indicates a purely informative question, while the absence of inversion is unmarked, and can indicate both a purely informative interrogative or one of the non-neutral types of questions to be discussed in Sections 5.2.2–5.2.5. In other words, inverted word order is marked.

5.2.2. Rhetorical questions

Rhetorical questions do not elicit information, but convey an opinion to the listener, or attempt to convince the listener of something. The implication of the rhetorical question is contrary to its literal denotation. In this type of question, or pseudo-question, the speaker uses negation as a rhetorical conversational strategy. Formal negation in rhetorical questions carries positive implicature, just as the lack of formal negation can carry negative implicature. Like negated informative Yes/No questions, negated rhetorical questions lack negative force. The interrogative particle *li* is used frequently.

(18) Nu,   **ne**   govoril **li**   ja tebe?

well NEG   told   Q   I you

'Well, didn't I tell you?!'

(19) Ljubil **li**   kto tebja, kak ja?

Loved Q   who you   as   I

'Did anyone love you like I did?!'

5.2.3. Dubious questions

Like formal negation in informative Yes/No questions and rhetorical questions, formal negation in dubious questions carries positive implicature. The speaker is unsure of the answer to the question being posed, but is assuming that it is the opposite of what is being said. In these questions, the particle *li* occurs frequently, as does the forced or optional pattern of expletive negation.

(20) **Ne**   vyzyvaet **li** tol'ko pobeda kadetov kakix-nibud'

NEG   cause   Q   only   victory cadets which-any$_{GEN}$

besporjadkov?

disturbances$_{GEN}$

'Could it be that the cadet victory is causing some disturbances?'

(21) **Ne** kroetsja **l i** pričina v čem-nibud' drugom?

NEG is-hidden Q reason in what-any other

'Could the reason be hidden somewhere else?'

= 'Maybe the reason is hidden/can be found somewhere else.'

(22) Už **ne** uznal **l i** kto-nibud' počemu ty ko mne xodiš'?

well NEG found-out Q who-any why you to me go

'Don't you think someone's found out why you come to my place?'

(23) Ty **ne** vykinula čego-nibud' bezrassudnogo?

you NEG tossed-out what-any imprudent

'You didn't spit anything out without thinking, did you?'

5.2.4. Presumptive questions

In this type of question the speaker is expecting a negative or positive answer. If the speaker is expecting a negative answer, then the question is negated and formal negation does carry negative implicature. The interrogative particle *li* is **disallowed** on the presumptive reading and the pattern of expletive negation does not occur.

(24) Vy verno **ne** zdešnie?

you probably NEG local

'You're not from around here, are you?'

(explicitly presumptive because of *verno*)

(25) Da vy, stalo byt', ničego **ne** zamečaete v sebe, **ni**

so you it-seems no-what NEG notice in self not

malejšego protivorečija?

[smallest contradiction]GEN

'So, it seems, you don't notice anything in yourself, not even the

smallest contradiction?'

(explicitly presumptive because of *stalo byt'*)

(26) Gnedič **ne** polučil moego pis'ma?

Gnedič NEG received [my letter]GEN

'Gnedich didn't receive my letter?'

(implicitly presumptive)

As Restan (1969) notes, the word order for presumptive Yes/No questions is always Subject-*ne*-Verb.

5.2.5. Questions as emotionally-charged responses

These questions express an emotional response, and in these types of questions, like the presumptive questions discussed in Section 5.2.4, formal negation carries negative implicature. The particle *li* is disallowed and the pattern of expletive negation is not observed.

(27) Kak? Ty ee **ne** našel?

how you her NEG found

'What, you didn't find her?!'

(28) A vy, jurist, **ne** znaete ètogo?

and you lawyer NEG know this

"And you, a lawyer, don't know this?!"

5.2.6. Summary

The table in (29) shows the classification of Russian Yes/No questions according to whether the negated variant carries negative implicature, whether *li* is allowed, and whether the pattern of expletive negation is observed.

(29) Classification of Russian Yes/No questions

Type of Question	Negative Implicature? (if negated)	*Li* Allowed?	Expletive Negation Observed
1. informative	–	√	√
2. rhetorical	–	√	√
3. dubious	–	√	√
4. presumptive	√	–	–
5. emotional	√	–	–

As we see in the table, those types of questions that do allow *li* can also exhibit the pattern of expletive negation when negated. However, we also see that not all formal and functional types of negated Yes/No questions in Russian allow the particle *li*. The occurrence of the *li* particle in *negated* Yes/No questions and the concomitant pattern of expletive negation is contingent on whether or not the given functional class is neutral or utilizes negative or positive form as a pragmatic strategy. Negated Yes/No questions without negative implicature do allow *li* and do exhibit this pattern. For example, negated **purely informative** Yes/No questions, which are pragmatically neutral, allow the particle *li* and exhibit this pattern. Negated Yes/No questions with negative implicature do not allow *li* and do not exhibit this pattern. Negated **presumptive** questions, which use negation to express the presumption of a negative answer, i.e., negative implicature, do not allow the particle *li* and do not exhibit the pattern of expletive negation. And, as mentioned in Section 5.1, even negated Yes/No questions not formed with the particle *li*, providing they fall into a functional class of interrogative that does allow *li*, also exhibit this pattern. Thus the pattern of expletive negation is in complementary distribution with negative implicature in Yes/No questions.

5.3. "Forced Expletive Negation": The Data

The pattern of expletive negation discussed in Section 5.1 always occurs when the particle *li* is present in a negated interrogative and forces movement of the [*ne* V] complex to C to host *li*, as in the purely informative question in (13) and the dubious question in (18). This pattern also always occurs in negated purely informative Yes/No questions without *li*, but with inversion, i.e., when the [*ne* V] complex raises to C, as shown in (30), where the NI-word is disallowed.[8,9]

---

[8] Recall that inversion in a non-*li* question marks a question as purely informative.

[9] Note that this sort of movement of negation has similar effects in English and French. Movement of the Neg head with the tensed verb to C in Yes/No questions prevents the occurrence in English of a strict NPI, such as *until*, as shown in (i).

(i)   *Didn't Mark start the Star Trek movie **until** Jay got there?

Compare this to the corresponding declarative in (ii), where negation licenses the NPI *until*.

(ii)   Mark didn't start the Star Trek movie **until** Jay got there

Also note that when negation does not move to C in (more formal) English, the NPI *until* is also fine, as in (iii).

(iii)   Did Mark **not** start the Star Trek movie **until** Jay got there?

Movement of negation in imperatives also does not restrict the occurrence of *until*, as in (iv).

(iv)   Do**n't** you start the Star Trek movie **until** Jay gets here.

Inversion in French, i.e., V-to-C movement, also prevents the occurrence of NPIs, as in (v), with the strict lexical NPI *lever le petit doigt* ('to lift a finger') rendered ungrammatical in a negated Yes/No question.

(v)   *N'   a-t- il   **pas** levé   le   petit   doigt?
        NEG   has he   not lifted   the   little   finger
        'Didn't he lift a finger?'

Note that the parallel NPI in English *to lift a finger* is not a strict NPI. In other words, it is licensed in all polarity contexts, not just clausemate negation. For this reason, the gloss to (v) is grammatical. Compare (v) to the declarative in (vi), where this NPI is fine with true clausemate negation.

(vi)   Il   **n'** a   **pas** levé   le   petit   doigt.
        he   NEG has NO lifted   the   little   finger
        'He didn't lift a finger.'

Thanks to Laurent Dekydtspotter for the latter example.

(30) **N e**   znaet ***nikto/kto-nibud'** iz vas, kak èto delaetsja?

    NEG   know *no-who/who-any   of you how this is-done

    'Do any of you know how this is done?'

The fact that pragmatically these types of questions cannot be presumptively negative suggests that movement of negation to C somehow results in negation being stripped of or lacking negative force and this accounts for the pattern of expletive negation. This is supported by the fact that in presumptively negative questions, which retain negative force, movement of negation to C must not occur and the pattern of expletive negation is not exhibited. Recall that the pattern of expletive negation can also occur in a negated interrogative without *li* and without movement of negation to C, but only if the negated interrogative does not carry negative implicature, as in (23). This suggests that it is the nature of negation in a given type of interrogative that results in this curious pattern, and that the syntactic pattern of expletive negation reflects the pragmatic use of negation in the interrogative in which it occurs.

In the remainder of this chapter I will investigate what it is about negated questions with movement of negation to C that forces expletive negation and results in the asymmetric pattern of grammaticality for NI-words and GN associated with it. The results of this investigation will account for why this pattern can be observed in non-*li* questions, where negation does not move to C, that lack negative implicature, but not for those with negative implicature.

Before turning to this analysis, I would like to provide one further piece of evidence that movement of negation to C is what forces expletive negation, namely "focal interrogation" (cf. King 1994a). In examples of focal interrogation, a non-verbal element is questioned, and not the verb, and the questioned constituent, rather than the [*ne* V] complex, raises to C^0 to host the interrogative particle *li*. Such Yes/No interrogatives contain *li* but do not exhibit the pattern of expletive negation. While such examples are stylistically awkward, given the conflict between fronted focus and the focusing of the NI-word, the following examples from B&F (1995: 221) seem relatively acceptable.

(31) a. V ètom **li** klube vy **ni** odnoj devočki **ne**   znaete?

        In this Q club you not [one girl]$_{GEN}$ NEG know

        'Is it in this club that you don't know a single girl?'

    b. V ètom **li**   magazine vy **ne**   našli **nikakogo** podarka?

        In this Q   store   you NEG   found [no-which gift]$_{GEN}$

        'Is it in this store that you didn't find a gift?'

c. Maše   **li**   vy   **ničego ne**   kupili?

Masha$_{DAT}$ Q   you no-what NEG   bought?

'Is it Masha that you didn't buy anything for?'

In these examples, *ne* has not raised to C. These examples show that it is not the presence of *li* alone in a negated clause that results in forced expletive negation, but rather the movement of the [*ne* V] complex to C to host *li*. We see in the examples in (32), where [*ne* V] does raise to C, that the NI-words are disallowed.

(32) a. ***Ne**   znaete **li** vy   v ètom   klube   **ni**   odnoj devočki

     NEG   know Q you in this   club   not [one   girl]$_{GEN}$

     ?'Do you not know a single girl in this club or not?'

   b. ***Ne** našli **li** vy   v ètom   magazine   **nikakogo**   podarka dlja

     NEG   found Q you in this   store   [no-which   gift]$_{GEN}$ for

     Vali?

     Valja

     ?'Did you find no gift in this store for Valja or not?'

   c. ***Ne**   kupili   **li**   vy   Maše   **ničego**?

     NEG   bought   Q   you Masha$_{DAT}$ nothing

     ?'Did you buy Masha nothing or not?'

5.4. Forced Expletive Negation: The Proposal

The present proposal is couched in the Minimalist framework of feature checking and the prohibition against feature mismatch, and exploits the similarities between Yes/No interrogation and negation, namely their status as polarity environments. This analysis treats the features associated with sentential negation and Yes/No interrogation as representing two distinct variants of a polarity feature [POL], as shown in (33) and (34), where [Q] in (34) is equivalent to [POS/NEG].

(33)   Sentential Negation

       [POL]
        |
       [NEG]

(34)   Yes/No Interrogation

       [POL]
        |
        [Q]

I borrow this type of feature decomposition from Bonet's (1995) discussion of morphology, from Generalized Phrase Structure Grammar's representation of features (Gazdar 1982, Gazdar, Klein, Pullum, and Sag 1983), and from phonological feature geometry (Clements 1985, Sagey 1986, Mester 1986, McCarthy 1988), whereby features can take other features as their values, and extend this notion to these syntactic features. This is akin to a type of feature redundancy rule, in that the presence of [NEG] or [Q] always indicates the presence of [POL] (but crucially not vice versa). This type of feature geometry allows for the existence of a [POL] feature with no features attached as well. Such a feature of course will have to be interpreted in some way, as we shall see.

5.4.1. The Feature [POL] and Negation

What we must account for in the following analysis is the asymmetric behavior of negation outlined above. In other words, we must explain why negation in contexts of true sentential negation licenses both NI-words and GN, while negation in certain types of negated interrogatives allows only GN, even though both types of clauses contain the negative marker *ne*.

In order to account for this behavior, I claim that the negative marker *ne* enters the derivation with the [POL] feature in its sublabel. Extending the notion of feature optionality discussed with respect to Genitive of Negation in Chapter 4 to these geometric complex features, I claim that the [POL] feature associated with the negative marker *ne* can have attached to it the feature [NEG], as in (33), or no feature at all. I propose that the feature [POL]-[NEG] is necessary to license the NI-words, and that some polarity feature *nondistinct* from this feature is necessary to license GN. Let us demonstrate how this might work.

5.4.1.1. Sentential Negation

First of all, it is important to show how such a feature will account for the NI-words, which require true sentential negation. I have assumed up to this point that in order for these pronouns to be licit, they must check and erase the feature [NEG] in their sublabel. I maintain this assumption here. Suppose that we take a numeration containing a NI-word as well as the negative marker *ne*. Suppose further that this negative marker contains in its sublabel the feature [POL] with the feature [NEG] attached. Let us derive the grammatical sentence given in (35).

(35) Ja **nikogo ne**   videl.

I   no-who NEG   saw

'I didn't see anyone.'

In (35) the NI-word *nikogo* ('no one') must raise to [Spec, NegP] to check its uninterpretable [NEG] feature. This is shown in (36).[10]

---

[10]Note that this can also involve covert raising of the feature [NEG] at LF, in

(36)   Checking of [NEG] in the Sublabel of *nikogo*

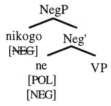

This type of configuration also accounts for the occurrence of GN on the argument *besporjadkov* in (37).

(37)   Pobeda kadetov **ne**   vyzyvaet **besporjadkov**.

victory of-cadets NEG   cause   disturbances$_{GEN}$

'The cadet victory is not causing disturbances.'

Here V raising to Neg to host *ne* creates a GN checking domain, given the presence in the feature sublabel of Neg^{0max} of the features [+V^{max}] and [POL]–[NEG] as shown in (38) and discussed in Chapter 4.

(38)   Checking of GN on *besporjadkov*

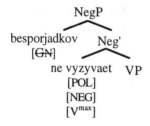

Given the fact that the presence of the [NEG] feature with sentential negation can account for both the NI-words, which requires the polarity feature [POL]–[NEG] as well as GN, which requires a polarity feature *nondistinct* from this feature, how do we explain the distribution of these negation sensitive phenomena in contexts of expletive negation?

5.4.1.2. Expletive Negation in Yes/No Questions

Just as the negative marker *ne* contains the feature [POL] with the feature [NEG] attached in sentences containing true sentential negation, the

---

which case only the feature will move to head-adjoin to the sublabel of the negative head *ne*, as in (5c) in Chapter 2. This would result in the NI-word remaining *in situ* as in (i):

(i)   Ja   **ne** videl **nikogo**

I   NEG saw   no-who

'I didn't see anyone.'

interrogative particle *li* contains the feature [POL] with the feature [Q] attached, as shown in (34). These two features are distinct features. This distinctiveness causes the incompatibility of negated Yes/No *li*-interrogatives and NI-words illustrated in (39).

(39) **N e**   vyzyvael **i** pobeda   kadetov   **kakix-nibud'/*nikakix**

   NEG   cause   Q victory   of-cadets   [which-any/*no-which

   besporjadkov?

   disturbances]$_{GEN}$

   'Could it be that the cadet victory is causing disturbances?'

In order to account for this, I follow the intuition in Brown 1995a, 1996b and B&F 1995 that what causes the ungrammaticality of such sentences as (39) is the raising of the [*ne*+V] complex to host *li* phonologically and the concomitant illegal interaction between true negation and interrogation. The two features, [POL]-[NEG], which is required for NI-words, and [POL]-[Q], are distinct polarity features that end up in a checking relation in these types of questions once the [*ne* V] complex raises to C, and this is what causes the derivation to crash. This is shown in (40) and (41). In (40) *nikakix besporjadkov* has raised to [Spec, Neg] in order to check the [NEG] feature of the NI-word against the [POL]-[NEG] feature of the negative head.

(40)   Checking of [NEG] on *nikakix (besporjadkov)*

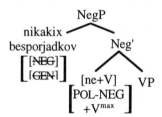

Once the derivation reaches the level of CP, the complex head [*ne vyzyvael*] raises to host the clitic *li* which serves as the head of CP, as in (41) on the following page. There the [*ne*+V] complex raises to head-adjoin to *li* as is shown in the circled area in the tree structure. Notice however, that the sublabel of C^{0max} now contains the mismatching features [POL]—[NEG] and [POL]—[Q]. This causes the derivation to crash. Therefore, what is necessary to license the NI-word *nikakix* in (39) above also causes a feature mismatch once the [*ne*+V] complex reaches C, hence the incompatibility of negated *li*-interrogatives and true sentential negation.

(41)   Raising of *ne vyzyvaet* to host *li*

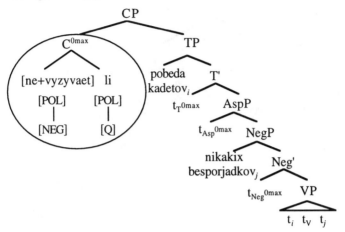

Now that we have accounted for the ungrammaticality of a NI-word in a negated *li*-question, how do we accommodate the fact that Genitive of Negation is grammatical in such structures? At this point I take advantage of the fact that in the Minimalist program all features are optional and certain universal principles ensure that only the correct derivation reaches the interface levels. What I propose is that the only licit option for negation in Yes/No questions that exhibit the pattern of Expletive Negation is for the feature [POL] to occur in the sublabel of *ne* without any feature value specified. In other words, there is no [NEG] attached to it. The ability of this feature to check Genitive of Negation lies in the fact that GN requires only a polarity feature *nondistinct* from [POL]—[NEG]. For this reason, the nondistinct [POL] that occurs in expletive contexts counts for purposes of checking GN. This is shown in (42) (cf. (40) above).

(42)   GN checking by [POL]

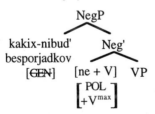

After GN has been checked by the polarity feature, the [*ne*+V] complex raises further to host *li*, as in (43) (cf. (41) above).

(43) [ne V] raises to host *li*

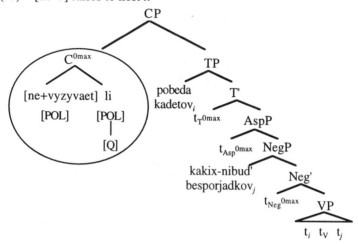

The checking configuration in the circled area that is established once [*ne* V] reaches C in (43) does not cause a feature mismatch. While [POL] alone is nondistinct from [POL]—[NEG] for purposes of GN checking, it is also nondistinct from [POL]—[Q] in the sublabel of *li* for purposes of feature matching.

However, as I mentioned before, this [POL] feature must be identified. I propose that this is achieved in a checking relation with some contentful polarity feature. This is exactly what we find in a Yes/No question. The unattached feature [POL] in the sublabel of *ne* occurs in a checking relation with the feature [POL]—[Q] in the sublabel of *li*, once it head-adjoins to host *li* phonologically. This accounts for why random generation of *ne* with only the [POL] feature does not occur. In order for *ne* to occur without the feature [NEG], it must be licensed and identified by some non-distinct polarity feature, such as the [POL]—[Q] feature in the sublabel of an interrogative C.

From this it follows why NI-words are disallowed in expletive contexts, while GN is perfectly acceptable. The NI-words require a polarity feature *identical* to [POL]—[NEG], while GN only requires a polarity feature *nondistinct* from it. This also explains why presumptive questions such as (12) above, repeated here as (44), are fine with NI-words.

(44) **A nikogo drugogo** iz podpol'scikov ty **ne** znaeš'?

and no-who other of undergrounders you NEG know

'So you don't know anyone else from the underground?'

Since the [*ne* V] complex never raises to C, where presumably there is a non-overt equivalent of *li* to indicate interrogativity, no feature mismatch results between the [POL]—[Q] feature of C and the [POL]—[NEG] feature of *ne*. The NI-word can check its [NEG] feature against the [POL]—[NEG] feature of *ne*, as in (40) above, and the sentence is interpreted as a presumptively negative Yes/No Question.

In addition this account provides an explanation for the optional occurrence of the pattern of expletive negation in negated questions without *li* and without movement of negation to C discussed in Sections 5.1 and 5.3. Compare (11), repeated as (45), with (44) above.

(45)   A   **kogo-nibud'**   drugogo iz   podpol'ščikov   ty   **ne**   znaeš'?

and who-any   other   of   undergrounders you NEG   know

'So do you know anybody else from the underground?

Here the negative marker is "optionally" generated without the [NEG] feature attached to its [POL] feature, and for this reason, the pattern of expletive negation occurs. The [POL] feature then raises at LF to be identified in a checking relation with the [POL]—[Q] feature in C. These are interpreted as non-presumptive Yes/No questions.

In cases of canonical (lexical) expletive negation, I simply claim that certain lexical items select a *ne* marked with the feature [POL] in its sublabel, that does not have the feature [NEG] necessary for licensing NI-words attached.

(46)   On boitsja, kak by   **kto-nibud'/*nikto ne**   narušit

he fears   how MOD who-any/ *no-who NEG   ruin

èksperimenta.

experiment$_{GEN}$

He's afraid someone might ruin the experiment.'

This accounts for why GN is allowed in (46), but the NI-word is not.[11]

5.5. Conclusion

In this chapter I discussed the asymmetric distribution of NI-words and Genitive of Negation in sentences containing canonical expletive negation. I showed that this pattern is also obligatory in negated Yes/No questions with the interrogative clitic *li* that forces [*ne*+V]-to-C movement and optional in other types of negated Yes/No questions as long as they do not contain negative implicature. I explained this by positing that the interaction of

---

[11] Notice that the facts presented here also suggest that we are dealing with syntactic movement of ne+V to C to host *li*, rather than prosodic inversion, i.e., *li* reordering at PF. Were prosodic inversion to be involved, we could not account for the expletive negation effects observed in *li*-questions. Thanks to Želko Bošković for bringing this to my attention.

negation and interrogation in such questions prevents negation from having true negative force.

Interrogation and negation consist only of polarity features on heads. Interrogatives are distinguished by the presence of a feature [Q] attached to [POL], and negation by the feature [NEG]. In order to account for the distribution of GN and NI-words, I suggested that a feature identical to [POL]—[NEG] is required to license NI-words, while only a feature nondistinct from [POL]—[NEG] is necessary for GN.

The proposed analysis not only handles the syntactic patterns observed for NI-words and GN that are associated with expletive negation in both canonical and (forced or optional) interrogative contexts, it accommodates the various functions and forms of negated interrogatives as well. Negated purely informative, dubious, and rhetorical Yes/No questions allow *li*, allow movement of negation to C even without *li*, and in both cases exhibit the pattern of expletive negation, because the negative marker *ne* lacks the negative feature [NEG]. Negated presumptive and emotionally charged questions, on the other hand, contain the negative feature, and for this reason are incompatible with *li* and the pattern of expletive negation and are restricted to Subj-*ne*-V word order.

Chapter 6: Expressing Negation

6.0. Introduction

In this monograph, I have attempted to show how negation facts in Russian can be accounted for by positing an abstract negative feature [NEG] that enters a derivation under the Neg^0 node and is overtly realized as the negative marker *ne*. In Chapter 1, I introduced the relevant negation phenomena from Russian and followed that in Chapter 2 with a practical introduction to the basic claims of the most recent published version of the Minimalist Program (Chomsky 1995) that are relevant throughout the subsequent chapters. In Chapter 3, in order to account for Negative Concord facts in Russian, I claimed that the [NEG] feature of negative constituents must be checked and erased in order for the sentence to receive a Negative Concord interpretation. This leaves only one feature expressing negation: the [NEG] feature of the negative head. In certain languages that exhibit Negative Concord, the negative constituents have [–Interpretable] NEG-features that *must* be checked off and erased in order for the derivation containing them to converge; this accounts for the obligatory NC reading in those languages. These include Russian. In Russian the [NEG] feature of the NI-words is uninterpretable and must be checked against the head of NegP, which in Russian is always overtly manifested as *ne*. In Chapter 4 I showed how the abstract feature [NEG] accounts for Genitive of Negation by creating a checking domain for GN together with the intrinsic verbal feature [V^{max}]. The combination of these features attracts the closest GN-marked DP in the structure, which can raise overtly to [Spec, NegP] or have just its feature sublabel raise covertly to head-adjoin to the feature sublabel of the negative head. This establishes a checking relation for GN, and eliminates the GN feature on the DP. In Chapter 5 I argued that expletive negation can also be accounted for by using the [NEG] feature. I showed how the feature [NEG] (attached to a [POL] feature) can account for the asymmetry observed in the distribution of GN and NI-words in contexts of true sentential negation and expletive negation, in particular negated Yes/No questions. In this concluding chapter, I will show how data from partitive expressions used to support arguments for the existence of a Neg-Op in Brown and Franks 1995 can also be accommodated by and provide further support for the [NEG] feature as the sole "expressor of negation".

6.1. Neg-Op and Partitive Expressions (from Brown and Franks 1995)

As support for the existence of NegP with a null Neg-Op in its Spec position, we presented in Brown and Franks 1995 evidence from Russian partitive expressions. We suggested that the null quantifier assigning partitive Genitive (Part-Gen) to the following material in (1) could occur only in the scope of some other element that licenses the empty Q and identifies it for proper interpretation.

(1)   Partitive Genitive

Normally the partitive occurs only after certain verbs, which Franks and Dziwirek (1993) explain by saying that a verb allowing a partitive complement must have a feature [+Qu] to identify the null quantifier (cf. Pesetsky 1982, Fowler 1987 and Neidle 1988, where similar claims are made). Thus the perfective verb *vypit'* ('to drink up$_{PERF}$') allows a complement in Part-Gen, but *s"est'* ('to eat up$_{PERF}$') does not. Compare (2a) and (2b) from Klenin 1978 based on Padučeva 1974:

(2)   a.   On   vypil   čaj/čaju.

             he   drank   tea$_{ACC/PART-GEN}$

             'He drank the tea/some tea.'

       b.   On   s"el   sup/*supu.

             he   ate   soup$_{ACC/*PART-GEN}$

             'He ate the soup/*some soup.'

Note that the partitive form in *-u* is highly restricted; Fowler (1987: 416) counts only 392 Russian nouns with a distinct partitive form. The regular Gen form can always be used in partitive contexts, even where a partitive in *-u* exists.

Based on the examples in (2) we concluded that *vypil* ('drank') but not *s"el* ('ate') contains the feature [+Qu] and therefore licenses the null Q of partitive phrases (cf. (1)). However, as Klenin notes, the imperfective *pit'* ('to drink$_{IMPERF}$') does not license the partitive, as in (3):

(3)   On pil   čaj/*čaju.

        he   drank   tea$_{ACC/*PART-GEN}$

        'He drank tea.'

Based on these examples we concluded that even the [+Qu] feature of the verb must also be activated by being in the scope of perfective aspect. Thus in the structure in (4) modified from Brown and Franks 1995, with the VP embedded in an AspP, a [+Qu] V must be minimally c-commanded by a [+Pf] Asp.

(4)   Basic Negated Clause Structure ((12) in B&F 1995)

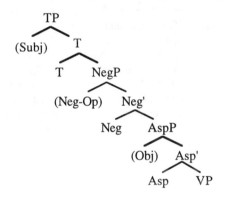

Negation, as Klenin (1978: 175) goes on to observe, mitigates the aspectual effect observed in (3), as shown in (5):

(5)   On ne   pil   čaj/čaja/čaju.

        he   NEG   drank   tea$_{ACC/GEN/PART-GEN}$

        'He didn't drink the tea/any tea.'

Based on this example we argued that the Neg-Op associated with *ne*, like perfective aspect, could also activate the [+Qu] feature on the imperfective verb *pil*. We claimed that, in more general terms, the [+Qu] feature of the verb which identifies the null Q of the partitive phrase must be in the scope of some kind of quantificational operator, and both negation and perfective aspect can serve this purpose. As further support that the interaction of negation and partitivity calls for a Neg-Op, we offered (6), in which the Yes/No Interrogative Operator (Int-Op) induces the same effect; the partitive is licensed with the imperfective verb *pil*.

(6)   Pil   li on   čaj/čaja/čaju?

     drank Q he   tea$_{\text{ACC/GEN/PART-GEN}}$

     'Did he drink (the) tea/any tea?'

We suggested that Neg-Op is thus on a par with the Int-Op required for the Yes/No question in (6). As we will see below, the data presented in this section, that were used in Brown and Franks 1995 as support for the presence of Neg-Op, can also be handled by an abstract [NEG] feature on the negative head.

6.2. [NEG] and Partitive Expressions

In order to show how the feature [NEG] can license partitive expressions, it is necessary to recall that the V containing the [+Qu] feature will move up through the various functional categories in order to check the features in its sublabel and pick up any enclitics. These include AspP, where head-adjunction to the head of Asp can "trigger" this feature if Asp contains [+PERFECTIVE] in its sublabel. This also includes NegP. I suggest that, rather than occurring in the c-command domain of a Neg-Op (or [PERFECTIVE]), the [+Qu] feature must be "checked", just as Case or Agreement features are checked. Note that in negated structures, such as (5), the verb containing the [+Qu] feature head-adjoins to Neg in order to host *ne*, which contains in its feature sublabel the feature [POL]—[NEG]. This head-adjunction creates a checking domain for the feature [+Qu] in the sublabel of the verb, shown here as (7) for the verb *pit'* ('to drink').[1]

(7)   Head-adjunction of V to Neg

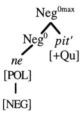

Since V moves through Asp, Neg, and possibly an interrogative C, the heads of these functional categories all contain features in their sublabels

---

[1] Notice that in (7) I have the negative head preceding the verb in this head-adjunction structure in order to account for the surface linear order, where *ne* always precedes the verb.

capable of "checking" or "triggering" the [+Qu] feature on the partitive verb.[2]

6.3. Expressing Negation

The goal of this work has been to present a Minimalist analysis of sentential and expletive negation in Russian that can also be extended to other languages. In Chapter 3, I presented an analysis of the NI-words, which exhibit Negative Concord, and extended this analysis to other languages discussed in the literature that also exhibit Negative Concord. In Chapter 4, I turned to the licensing mechanisms for Genitive of Negation, the optional Case marking of an internal argument of a negated verb. In Chapter 5, I discussed the asymmetric pattern observed between the NI-words and GN in contexts of expletive negation, i.e., in lexicalized expressions and in negated Yes/No questions with and without the particle *li*. There I transformed the abstract negation feature of Chapters 3 and 4 into a polarity feature with a [NEG] feature attached. I concluded that the NI-words require the [NEG] feature, while GN only requires a polarity feature nondistinct from this feature. This excluded NI-words in contexts of expletive negation, which necessarily lack the [NEG] feature. In this Chapter, I extended the analysis to show how it accounts for data from partitive expressions. Based on the evidence and the analysis presented, I conclude that what "expresses negation" is an abstract feature [NEG] that enters a derivation as a Neg head; in the case of Russian, this Neg head is always overt, while in languages like Italian it is overt only if it has to be.

---

[2]Note that this also unifies the feature [NEG] with the feature [Q] and the feature [PERFECTIVE]. In B&F 1995, the former two were operators, while the latter was a head.

References

Acquaviva, P. 1992. The representation of negative'quantifiers'. *Rivista di Linguistica* 4, 319-381.

_____. 1993. *The logical form of negation: A study of operator-variable structures in syntax.* Doctoral Dissertation, Scuola Normale Superiore, Pisa.

Adamec, P. 1991. *Porjadok slov v sovremennom russkom jazyke.* Prague: Academia.

Aksenov, V. P. 1994. *Sobranie sočinenii.* Moskva: Junost'.

Aoun, J. 1985. *A grammar of anaphora.* Cambridge, Mass.: MIT Press.

_____. 1986. *Generalized binding.* Dordrect: Foris.

Aoun, J., N. Hornstein, D. Lightfoot, and A. Weinberg 1987. Two types of locality. *Linguistic Inquiry* 18, 537-577.

Aoun, J., N. Hornstein, and D. Sportiche 1980. Some aspects of wide scope quantification, *Journal of Linguistic Research* 1.3, 96-95.

Aoun, J., and D. Sportiche 1983. On the formal theory of government. *The Linguistic Review* 3, 211-235.

Babby, L. 1980a. *Existential sentences and negation in Russian.* Ann Arbor: Karoma.

_____. 1980b. Word order, case, and negation in Russian existential sentences. In *Slavic transformational syntax*, edited by R. Brecht and C. Chvany, 221-234. Columbus: Slavica.

_____. 1984. Prepositional quantifiers and the direct case condition in Russian. In *Issues in Russian morphosyntax*, edited by R. Brecht and M. Flier, 91-117. Columbus, Ohio: Slavica Publishers.

_____. 1987. Case, prequantifiers, and discontinuous agreement in Russian. *Natural Language and Linguistic Theory* 5, 91-138.

Bailyn, J. 1995a. Underlying phrase structure and short verb movement in Russian. *Journal of Slavic Linguistics* 3.1, 13-58.

_____. 1995b. *A Configurational approach to Russian 'free' word order.* Doctoral Dissertation, Cornell University, Ithaca, NY.

_____. 1997. Genitive of negation is obligatory. In *Formal approaches to Slavic linguistics: The Cornell meeting*, edited by W. Browne, E. Dornisch, and D. Zec, 84-114. Ann Arbor, Mich.: Michigan Slavic Publishers.

Baker, C. 1970. Problems of polarity in counter-factuals. In *Studies presented to Robert B. Lees by his students*, edited by J. Sadock and A. Vanek, 1-15. Carbondale/Edmonton: Linguistic Research.

Baker, M. 1988. *Incorporation: A theory of grammatical function changing.* Chicago: University of Chicago Press.

Beard, Robert 1995. *Lexeme-morpheme base morphology: a general theory of inflection and word formation.* Albany, NY: State University of New York Press.

Belletti, A. 1988. The case of unaccusatives. *Linguistic Inquiry* 19, 1-34.

Beletti, A., and L. Rizzi. 1981. The syntax of 'ne': some theoretical implications. *The Linguistic Review* 1, 117-154.

Billings, L. 1995. *Approximation in Russian and the single-word constraint.* Ph. D. Dissertation, Princeton University.

Bonet, E. 1995. On the internal feature structure of Romance pronominal clitics. *Natural Language and Linguistic Theory* 13.4, 607-647.

Borer, H. 1993. The projection of arguments. In *U Mass occasional papers in linguistics* (UMOP) 17, 19-48. Amherst, Mass.: University of Massachusetts.

Borkovksij, V., and P. Kuznecov. 1965. *Istoričeskaja grammatika russkogo jazyka.* Moskva: Nauka.

Borovikova, N. 1996. Negated adjunct phrases are REALLY the genitive of negation. Paper presented at Formal Approaches to Slavic Linguistics V, Crawfordsville, Indiana.

Bošković, Ž. To appear. WH-movement in Slavic. To appear in proceedings of *Workshop on Comparative Slavic Morphosyntax*, Indiana University, June 1998.

Bouchard, D. 1984. *On the content of empty categories.* Dordrecht: Foris.

Bowers, J. 1994. The syntax of predication. *Linguistic Inquiry* 24.4, 591-656.

Brody, M. 1993. *Lexico-logical form – a radically minimalist theory.* Cambridge, Mass.: MIT Press.

Brown, S. 1995a. Scope of negation: Genitive of negation and polarity in Russian. *Proceedings of the Formal Linguistics Society of Mid-America* 6.2, 13-24.

_____. 1995b. The status of Russian pronouns in -*nibud'*. Talk given at AATSEEL, Chicago.

_____. 1996a. Negative concord in Russian. Paper presented at Formal approaches to Slavic linguistics V.

_____. 1996b. *The syntax of negation in Russian.* Doctoral Dissertation, Indiana University, Bloomington.

_____. To appear. Negative concord and attract all. To appear in proceedings of *Workshop on Comparative Slavic Morphosyntax*, Indiana University, June 1998.

Brown, S., and S. Franks. 1995. Asymmetries in the scope of Russian negation. *Journal of Slavic Linguistics* 3.2, 239-287.

_____. 1997. The syntax of pleonastic negation in Russian. In *Formal approaches to Slavic linguistics IV: The Cornell Meeting*, edited by W. Browne, E. Dornisch, N. Kondrashova, and D. Zec, 135-164. Ann Arbor, Mich.: Michigan Slavic Publishers.

Bunin, I. 1980. Porjadok slov. In *Russkaja grammatika* 2, edited by N. Švedova. Nauka: Moscow.

Burzio, L. 1986. *Italian syntax.* Dordrect: Reidel.

Carlson, G. 1980. 'Polarity *any* is existential. *Linguistic Inquiry* 11, 799-804.

Catell, R. 1976. Constraints on movement rules. *Language* 52, 18-50.

Cheng, L. L.-S. 1991. *On the typology of WH-questions*. Doctoral Dissertation, MIT, Cambridge, Mass.

Chomsky, N. 1965. *Aspects of the theory of syntax*. Cambridge, Mass.: MIT Press.

————. 1972. *Studies on semantics in generative grammar*. The Hague: Mouton.

————. 1981. *Lectures on government and binding*. Dordrecht: Foris.

————. 1986. *Barriers*. Cambridge, Mass.: MIT Press.

————. 1991. Some notes on economy of derivation and representation. In *Principles and parameters in comparative grammar*, edited by R. Friedin, 417-454. Cambridge, Mass.: MIT Press.

————. 1992. A minimalist program for linguistic theory. In *The view from building 20: Essays in linguistics in honor of Sylvain Bromberger*, edited by M. Hale and S. Keyser, 1-52. Cambridge, Mass.: MIT Press.

————. 1994. Bare phrase structure. *MIT occasional papers in linguistics* 5. Department of Linguistics and Philosophy, MIT, Cambridge Mass.

————. 1995. *The minimalist program*. Cambridge, Mass.: MIT Press.

————. 1997. MIT Class Lectures.

Chomsky, N. & H. Lasnik. 1993. The theory of principles and parameters. In *Syntax: An international handbook of contemporary research*, edited by J. Jacobs, A. von Stechow, W. Sternefeld, and T. Vennemann, 506-569. Berlin: de Gruyter.

Chung, S., and J. McCloskey. 1983. On the interpretation of certain island facts in GPSG. *Linguistic Inquiry* 14, 700-713.

Chvany, C. 1975. *On the syntax of BE-sentences in Russian*. Cambridge, Mass.: Slavica Publishers.

Cinque, G. 1991. *Types of A-bar dependencies*. Cambridge, Mass.: MIT Press.

Clements, G. N. 1985. The geometry of phonological features. *Phonology yearbook* 2, 225-252.

Cole, P., G. Hermon, and L.-M. Sung. 1990. Principles and parameters of long-distance reflexives. *Linguistic Inquiry* 21.1, 1-22.

Comrie, B. 1980. Clause structure and movement constraints in Russian. In *Slavic transformational syntax*, edited by R. Brecht and C. Chvany, 98-113. Slavica.

Corbett, G. 1986. The use of the genitive or accusative for the direct object of negated verbs in Russian: A bibliography. In *Case in Slavic*, edited by R. Brecht and J. Levine, 361-172. Columbus, OH: Slavica.

Crockett, D. 1977. The scope of denial in Russian negative sentences. *Lingua* 43, 229-245.

Culicover, P. and W. Wilkins. 1984. *Locality in linguistic theory*. New York: Academic Press.

Diesing, M. 1992. *Indefinites*. Cambridge, Mass.: MIT Press.

Diesing, M., and E. Jelinek. 1995. Distributing arguments. *Natural Language Semantics* 2, 1-54.

Emonds, J. 1976. *A transformational approach to syntax.* New York: Academic Press.

Espinal, M. T. 1991. On expletive negation: Some remarks with regard to Catalan. *Lingvisticae investigationes: Revue internationale de linguistique francaise et de linguistique generale* 15 .1, 41-65.

_____. 1992. Expletive negation and logical absorption. *Linguistic Review* 9, 333-358.

Fowler, G. 1987. *The syntax of the genitive case in Russian.* Doctoral dissertation, University of Chicago.

_____. 1996. Oblique passivization in Russian. *Slavic and East European Journal* 40:3, 519-547.

Fowler, G., and M. Yadroff. 1993. The argument status of accusative measure nominals in Russian. *Journal of Slavic Linguistics* 1.2, 251-279.

Franks, S. 1986. Case and the structure of NP. In *Case in Slavic*, edited by Brecht, R. and J. Levine, 220-243. Columbus, OH: Slavica.

_____. 1990. Case, configuration and argumenthood: reflections on the second dative. *Russian Linguistics* 14, 231-254.

_____. 1995. *Parameters in Slavic morphosyntax.* Oxford: Oxford University Press.

Franks, S., and K. Dziwirek. 1993. Negated adjunct phrases are really partitive. *Journal of Slavic Linguistics* 1.2, 280-305.

Franks, S., and G. Greenberg. 1988. Agreement, tense, and the case of subjects in Slavic. *Chicago Linguistic Society, parasession on agreement* 24, 71-86.

Gazdar, G. 1982. *Phrase structure grammar.* Reidel: Dordrecht.

Gazdar, G., E. Klein, G. Pullum, and I. Sag (1983), "Foot features and parasitic gaps". In *Sentential complementation: Proceedings of the International Conference held at UFSAL, Brussels*, edited by Geest, W. de, Y. Putseys, H. van Riemsdijk, 83-94.

Greenberg, G. 1983. Another look at the second dative and related subjects. *Linguistic Analysis* 11, 167-218.

_____. 1988. Relativization and subjacency in Russian. *Proceedings of the Eastern states conference on linguistics* 5, 187-197.

Grevisse, M. 1988. *Le bon usage: Grammaire française.* Paris: Duculot, 12th ed.

Grœnendijk J., and M. Stokhof. 1989. Type-shifting rules and the semantics of interrogatives. In *Properties, types and meanings II*, edited by G. Chierchia, B. Partee, and R. Turner, 21-86. Dordrecht and Boston: Kluwer Academic Publishers.

Haegeman, L. 1992. Negation in West Flemish and the Neg Criterion. *Proceedings of the NELS conference, 22.*

_____. 1995. *The syntax of negation.* Cambridge: Cambridge University Press.

Haegeman L. and R. Zanuttini. 1990. Negative Concord in West Flemish. University of Geneva, Ms.

_____. 1991. Negative heads and the Neg criterion. *The Linguistic Review* 8, 233-52.

_____. 1996. Negative concord in West Flemish. In *Parameters and Functional Heads. Essays in Comparative Syntax*, edited by A. Belletti and L. Rizzi, 117-180. Oxford and New York: Oxford University Press.

Hale, K., and S. J. Keyser. 1993a. On argument structure and the lexical expression of syntactic relations. In *The view from building 20: Essays in linguistics in honor of Sylvain Bromberger*, edited by K. Hale and S. J. Keyser, 53-110. Cambridge, Mass.: MIT Press.

Heim, I. 1988. *The semantics of definite and indefinite noun phrases*. New York: Garland.

Higganbothom, J., and R. May. 1981. Questions, quantifiers, and crossing. *The Linguistic Review* 1, 41-79.

Horn, L. 1989. *A natural history of negation*. Chicago: University of Chicago Press.

Hornstein, N. 1995. *Logical form: From GB to minimalism*. Cambridge, Mass.: Blackwell.

Huang, C. T. J. 1982. Move WH in a language without WH movement. *The Linguistic Review* 1, 369-416.

Huang, C.-T. J., and C.-C. J. Tang. 1989. On the local nature of the long-distance reflexives in Chinese. *Proceedings of NELS* 19, 193-206.

Hyams, N., and S. Sigurjónsdóttir. 1990. The development of long-distance anaphora: a cross linguistic comparison with special reference to Icelandic. *Language Acquisition* 1, 57-93.

Isačenko, A. 1966. O grammatičeskom porjadke slov. *Voprosy jazykoznanija* 6, 27-34.

Jackendoff, R. 1977. *X'-syntax*. Cambridge, Mass.: MIT Press.

Jaeggli, O. 1980. *On some phonologically-null elements in syntax*. Doctoral Dissertation, MIT, Cambridge, Mass.

Jaeggli, O., and K. Safir. 1989. The null subject parameter and parametric theory. In *The null subject parameter*, edited by O. Jaeggli and K. Safir, 1-44. Dordrecht: Kluwer.

Jakobson, R. 1936. Beitrag zur allgemeinen Kasuslehre: Gesamtbedeutungen der russischen Kasus. *Selected writings*. The Hague: Mouton, v. 2, 23-71.

_____. 1958. Morfologičeskie nabljudenija nad slavjanskim skloneniem. in *Selected writings* 2, 154-182. The Hague: Mouton,

Kadmon, N., and F. Landman. 1993. Any. *Linguistics and Philosophy* 16, 353-422.

Kayne, R. 1983. Connectedness. *Linguistic Inquiry* 14, 223-249.

_____. 1984. *Connectedness and binary branching*. Dordrecht: Foris.

_____. 1994. *The antisymmetry of syntax*. Cambridge, Mass.: MIT Press.

Keil, R. 1970. Zur Wahl des Objektkasus bei verneinten Verben im modernen Russisch. *Zeitschrift für Slavische Philologie* 35, 109-133.

Kiklevič, A. 1990. Otricatel'nye mestoimeniia v utverditel'nom predloženii (na materiale russkogo i pol'skogo jazyka). *Filologičeskie nauki* 5, 114-119.

_____. 1992. Semantika absoljutnoj kvantifikacii v otricatel'nom predloženii. *Filologičeskie nauki* 4, 96-103.

King, T. 1993. *Configuring topic and focus in Russian*. Doctoral Dissertation, Stanford University.

_____. 1994a. Focus in Russian yes-no questions. *Journal of Slavic Linguistics* 2.1, 92-120.

_____. 1994b. The structure of Russian clausal negation. *Journal of Slavic Linguistics* 2.2, 287-297.

_____. 1994c. VP-internal subjects in Russian. In *Formal Approaches to Slavic Linguistics: The MIT Meeting*, edited by S. Avrutin, S. Franks, and Lj. Progovac, 216-234. Ann Arbor: Michigan Slavic Publications.

_____. 1995. *Configuring topic and focus in Russian*. Stanford: CSLI Publications.

Klenin, E. 1978. Quantification, partitivity, and the genitive of negation. *International Review of Slavic Linguistics* 3, 163-182.

Klima, E. 1964. Negation in English. In *Readings in the philosophy of language*, edited by J. A. Fodor and J. J. Katz, 246-332. Englewood Cliffs, N. J.: Prentice-Hall.

Koopman H., and D. Sportiche. 1982. Variables and the bijection principle. *The Linguistic Review* 2, 139-160.

Koster, J. 1984. On binding and control. *Linguistic Inquiry* 15, 417-459.

_____. 1987. *Domains and dynasties*. Dordrect: Foris.

Kovtunova, I. 1976. *Porjadok slov i aktual'noe členenie predloženija*. Moskva: Prosveščenie.

Kŕížková, H. 1968. K voprosy o tak nazyvaemoj dvojnoj negacii v slavjanskix jazykaz. *Slavia:Časopis pro Slovanskou Filologii* 37, 21-29.

Ladusaw, W. 1980. *Polarity sensitivity as inherent scope relations*. New York: Garland.

_____. 1992. Expressing negation. *Ohio State University Working papers in linguistics* 40, 237-59.

_____. 1994. Thetic and categorial, stage and individual, weak and strong. In *Salt IV Proceedings*. New York: University of Rochester.

Laka, I. 1990. *Negation in syntax: On the nature of functional categories and projections*. Doctoral dissertation, MIT, Cambridge, Mass.

Larson, R. 1988. On the double object construction. *Linguistic Inquiry* 19, 335-392.

Lasnik, H., and M. Saito. 1984. On the nature of proper government. *Linguistic Inquiriy* 15.2, 235-289.

124 / References

_____. 1992. *Move α.* Cambridge, Mass.: MIT Press.

Lasnik H., and J. Uriagereka. 1988. *A course in GB syntax.* Cambridge, Mass.: MIT Press.

Lebeaux, D. 1983. A distributional difference between reciprocals and reflexives. *Linguistic Inquiry* 14.4, 723-730.

Linebarger, M. C. 1981. *The grammar of negative polarity.* Bloomington: Indiana University Linguistics Club.

_____. 1987. Negative polarity and grammatical representation. *Linguistics and Philosophy* 10, 325-387.

Manzini, M. R. 1992. *Locality: A theory and some of its empirical consequences.* Cambridge, Mass.: MIT Press.

Manzini, R., and K. Wexler. 1987. Parameters, binding theory, and learnability. *Linguistic Inquiry* 24.3, 413-444.

May, R. 1985. *Logical form: Its structure and derivation.* Cambridge, Mass.: MIT Press.

McCarthy, J. 1988. "Feature geometry dependency: A review". *Phonetica* 43: 84-108.

Mester, R. 1986. *Studies in tier structure.* Doctoral Dissertation, University of Massachusetts. [Published by Garland Press, New York, 1988].

Mustajoki, A. 1985. *Padež dopolnenija v russkix otricatel'nyx predloženijax 1: Izyskanija novyx metodov v izučenii staroj problemy.* Slavica Helsingiensia 2. Helsinki: University Press.

Mustajoki, A., and H. Heino. 1991. *Case selection for the direct object in Russian negative clauses.* Slavica Helsingiensia 9. Helsinki: University Press.

Nam, S. 1994. Another type of negative polarity item. In *Dynamics, polarity and quantification,* edited by M. Kanazawa and C. Piñón, 3-16. Stanford, CA: CSLI Publications.

Neidle, C. 1988. *The role of case in Russian syntax.* Dordrect: Kluwer.

Ouhalla, J. 1991. *Functional categories and parametric variation.* London, New York: Routledge.

Padučeva, E. 1974. *O semantike sintaksisa.* Moscow: Nauka.

_____. 1985. *Vyskazyvanie i ego sootnesennost' s dejstvitel'nost'ju.* Moscow: Nauka.

Parsons, T. 1990. *Events in the semantics of English: a study in subatomic semantics.* Cambridge, Mass.: MIT Press.

Pesetsky, D. 1982. *Paths and categories.* Doctoral dissertation, MIT, Cambridge, Mass..

Pesetsky, D. 1987., *Wh*-in-situ: movement and unselective binding. In *The representation of (in)definiteness,* edited by E. Reuland and A. ter Meulen, 98-129. Cambridge, Mass.: MIT Press.

Pica, P. 1987. On the nature of the reflexivization cycle. *Proceedings of New England Linguistics Society* 17, 483-499.

Pigin, M. 1962. Iz istorii otritsatel'nyx bezličnyx predloženii v russkom jazyke. *Lingvističeskii sbornik* 1, 16-45.

Piñon, C. 1993. ΣP and Hungarian. In *Proceedings of the eleventh West Coast Conference on Formal Linguistics* (WCCFL), edited by J. Mead, 388-404. Stanford, Calif.: CSLI Publications.

Pollock, J. -Y. 1989. Verb movement, universal grammar, and the structure of IP, *Linguistic Inquiry* 20, 365-424.

Progovac, Lj. 1988. *A binding approach to polarity sensitivity.* Doctoral Dissertation, University of Southern California, Los Angeles.

_____. 1990a. Free-choice *Bilo* in Serbo-Croatian: Existential or universal?. *Linguistic Inquiry* 21.1, 130-135.

_____. 1990b. Inversion as a purely structural phenomenon. In *Mid-America Linguistics Conference Papers*, 277-93. Lawrence, KS: University of Kansas.

_____. 1991. Polarity in Serbo-Croatian: Anaphoric NPIs and pronominal PPIs. *Linguistic Inquiry* 22.3, 567-72.

_____. 1992a. Relativized SUBJECT: long-distance reflexives without movement. *Linguistic Inquiry* 23.4, 671-80.

_____. 1992b. Non-negative polarity licensing must involve Comp. *Linguistic Inquiry* 23.2, 341-47.

_____. 1992c. Negative polarity: A semantic-syntactic approach. *Lingua* 86, 271-99.

_____. 1993a. Locality and subjunctive-like complements in Serbo-Croatian, *Journal of Slavic Linguistics* 1.1, 116-144.

_____. 1993b. Negative polarity: Entailment and binding. *Linguistics and Philosophy: An international journal* 16.2, 149-80.

_____. 1993c. Subjunctive: The (mis)behavior of anaphora and negative polarity. *The Linguistic Review* 10.1, 37-59.

_____. 1993d. Negation and Comp. *Rivistia di Linguistica* 5.2, 329-347.

_____. 1994. *Negative and positive polarity: A binding approach.* Cambridge: Cambridge University Press.

Radford, A. 1981. *Transformational Syntax: A student's guide to Chomsky's Extended Standard Theory.* Cambridge: Cambridge University Press.

_____. 1988. *Transformational grammar: a first course.* Cambridge: Cambridge University Press.

_____. 1997. *Syntactic theory and the structure of English: A minimalist approach.* Cambridge: Cambridge University Press.

Rappaport, G. 1986. On anaphor binding in Russian. *Natural Language and Linguistic Theory* 4, 97-120.

Ravich R. 1971. O vybore padeža prjamogo dopolnenija pri perexodnyx glagolax s otricaniem v russkom jazyke. *Fonetika. Fonologija. Grammatika. K semidesiatiletiju A. A. Reformatskogo.* 254-265.

Restan, P. 1969. *Sintaksis voprositel'nogo predloženija.* Oslo: Universitetsforlaget.

Rizzi, L. 1982. *Issues in Italian syntax.* Dordrecht: Foris.

_____. 1990. *Relativized minimality.* Cambridge, Mass.: MIT Press.

_____. 1996. Residual verb second and the WH criterion. In *Parameters and functional heads. Essays in comparative syntax,* edited by A. Belletti and L. Rizzi, 63-90. Oxford and New York: Oxford University Press.

Ross, J. 1967. *Constraints on variables in syntax.* Doctoral Dissertation, MIT, Cambridge, Mass.

Rudin, C. 1988b. Multiple questions in South Slavic, West Slavic, and Romanian. *Slavic and East European Journal* 32.1, 1-24.

_____. 1988a. On multiple questions and multiple WH fronting. *Natural Language and Linguistic Theory* 6.4, 445-501.

Sagey, E. 1986. *The representation of features and relations in non-linear phonology.* Doctoral Dissertation, Massachusetts Institute of Technology.Giannakidou, A., and J. Quer. 1995. The semantics of negative indefinites. In *Proceedings of Formal Linguistics Society of Mid-America* VI (2): 103-114.

Schein, B. 1982. Non-finite complements in Russian. *MIT working papers in linguistics* 4, 217-244.

Solonicyn, Ju. 1962. Nekotorye leksiko-grammatičeskie faktory, obuslovlivajuščie vybor padeža prjamogo dopolnenija pri otricanii. *Očerki po russkomu jazyku. Kirovskij gosudarstvennyj pedagogičeskij institut im. V. I. Lenina,* 99-116. Kirov.

Speas, M. 1994. Null arguments in a theory of projection. *Functional projections: University of Massachusetts occasional papers* 17, 179-208.

_____. 1995. Economy, agreement and the representation of null arguments. Ms., University of Massachusetts.

Strugackij, A., and B. Strugackij. 1993. *Sobranie sočinenij.* Moskva: Tekst.

Švedova, N. (ed.) 1980. *Russkaja grammatika* vol. 2. Moskva: Nauka.

Timberlake, A. 1975. Hierarchies in the genitive of negation. *Slavic and East European Journal* 19, 123-138.

_____. 1979. Reflexivization and the cycle in Russian. *Linguistic Inquiry* 10, 109-141.

Tomson, A. 1903. *K sintaksisu I semasiologii russkago iazyka.* Odessa: Ekonomicheskaia tip..

Travis, L. 1991. Derived objects, inner aspect, and the structure of VP. Unpublished paper given at NELS 1991, U. of Delaware.

Tsurikov, A. 1967. *Case selection in clauses with negative transitive verbs in contemporary Russian.* Doctoral dissertation: University of Rochester.

Uglitsky, Z. 1956. Accusative and genitive with transitive verbs preceded by a negative in contemporary Russian. *The Slavonic Review* 34, 1955/56, 377-87.

Vallduví, E. 1994. Polarity items, n-words, and minimizers in Catalan and Spanish. *Probus* 6, 263-294.

van der Wouden, T. 1994. Polarity and 'illogical negation'. In *Dynamics, polarity and quantification*, edited by M. Kanazawa and C. Piñón, 17-45. Stanford, CA: CSLI Publications.

Wexler, K., and R. Manzini. 1987. Parameters and learnability in binding theory. In *Parameter setting*, edited by T. Roeper and E. Williams, 41-76. Dordrect: Reidel.

Watanabe, A. 1991. WH-in-situ, subjacency, and chain formation. Ms., MIT.

Williams, E. 1977. Discourse and logical form. *Linguistic Inquiry* 8, 103-139.

Yadroff, M. 1994. AspP and licensing of *pro-arb* objects. *Proceedings of Western Conference on Linguistics* 7, 290-303.

Yokoyama, O. 1986. *Discourse and word order*. Philadelphia: John Benjamins.

Zanuttini, R. 1988. Two strategies for negation: Evidence from Romance. *Proceedings of Fifth ESCOL*.

_____. 1989. The structure of negative clauses in Romance. Ms., University of Pennsylvania.

_____. 1991. *Syntactic properties of sentential negation: A comparative study of Romance languages*. Doctoral Dissertation, University of Pennsylvania, Philadelphia.

Zanuttini, R. 1994. Reexamining negative clauses. In *Paths towards Universal Grammar: Studies in honor of Richard S. Kayne*, edited by G. Cinque, J. Koster, J.-Y. Pollock, L. Rizzi, R. Zanuttini, 427-451. Washington: Georgetown University Press.

Index

—B—

Billings, 24
Bonet, 106
Borer, 58
Borkovksij and Kuznecov, 2
Bošković, 8, 29, 67, 111
Bowers, 52, 56, 58, 60, 63, 70
Brown, 25, 49, 50, 53, 58, 67, 94, 97, 108. *See Also* Brown and Franks
Brown and Franks, 3, 25-26, 49-50, 53, 58-59, 84, 94, 96-97, 104, 108, 114-117
Browne, 34
Burzio's generalization, 72
  and passive verbs. *See* Verbs (Passive)
  and unaccusative verbs. *See* Verbs (Unaccusative)

—C—

Canonical Expletive Negation, 3, 4, 94-95, 97, 111-112. *See Also* čut' ne, poka ne. *See* Expletive Negation
  and Genitive of Negation, 4, 95-97, 111, 112
  and negative constituents, 4, 95-97, 111-112
Carson, 24
Case Alternations
  Accusative Case and Case alternations with Genitive of Negation. *See* Accusative Case
  Genitive of Negation and Case alternations. *See* Genitive of Negation
  Nominative Case and Case alternations with Genitive of Negation. *See* Nominative Case
Case Checking. *See* Checking of Case
  and Case features. *See* Features (Case Features)
  by Attract. *See* Attract
  by covert movement. *See* Covert Movement for Case Checking

by movement (general). *See* Movement (general) for Case Checking
  by overt movement. *See* Overt Movement for Case Checking
Case-checking feature complexes. *See* Case-checking Feature Complexes
  of Accusative. *See* Accusative Case
  of Genitive of Negation. *See* Genitive of Negation
  of Nominative Case. *See* Nominative Case
Case Features. *See* Features (Case Features)
  and Case-checking feature complexes. *See* Case-checking Feature Complexes
  checking of. *See* Checking of Case
    by Attract. *See* Attract for Case Checking
    by covert movement. *See* Covert Movement for Case Checking
    by movement (general). *See* Movement (general) for Case Checking
    by overt movement. *See* Overt Movement for Case Checking
Case Marking
  Accusative. *See* Accusative Case
  and Case checking. *See* Checking of Case
  and Case features. *See* Features (Case Features)
  and Case-checking feature complexes. *See* Case-checking Feature Complexes
  and negated copular structures, 85-89
  and transitive verbs, 65-69, 72, 74, 76-77, 79-81, 93
  and unaccusative verbs, 72-74, 82-84
  and unergative verbs, 70-71, 74, 81-82, 93
  Dative. *See* Dative Case

—D—

aspect features. *See* Features

Φ-features. *See* Features

negative feature [NEG]. *See*
Features

tense features. *See* Features

Functional Form, 57, 91

—G—

Gazdar, 106

Gazdar, Klein, Pullum, and Sag,
106

Generalized Phrase Structure
Grammar, 106

Generic Interpretation. *See Also*
Existential Interpretation,
Presuppositional Interpretation

and ACC-marked arguments, 48,
75

and NOM-marked arguments, 48-
49, 57-58, 92-93

and tree splitting, 57-58, 90,
92-93

Genitive of Negation, 5, 9, 13, 44,
45, 56, 58, 79, 112

and case alternations, 48, 75, 89

  with Accusative, 3, 47-48,
50, 60, 72, 75-76, 79, 81-
82, 84, 86

  with Nominative, 3, 47-48,
50, 60, 72, 75-76, 82, 85-
86, 88-89

and constituent negation, 50

and existential verbs, 45-48, 50,
60, 82, 93. *See Also* Genitive
of Negation and Negated
Copular Structures

and expletive negation, 3, 94,
106-107, 111, 114, 117

  canonical, 4, 95-97, 111-112

  forced, 4, 97, 104, 109-110,
112

  optional, 98, 112

and external arguments. *See*
Arguments

and impersonal verbs, 47

and incorrect Case marking, 81-
82

and negated copular structures,
60, 84-88, 93

and oblique objects, 45- 47, 51-
52, 62

and passive verbs, 47, 52

and polarity behavior, 42

and polarity feature [POL], 106-
107, 109-110

and quirky Case marking, 62

and scope of negation, 1, 49-51,
97

and transitive verbs, 2-3, 45-48,
50-51, 60, 72, 75-79, 81-82

and unaccusative verbs, 2-3, 45-
48, 51-52, 60, 72, 75-76, 82-
84

and unergative verbs, 2, 46-48,
51, 60, 76, 81-82

as diagnostic for sentential
negation, 1-2, 18, 95, 97,
106

assignment of

  under existential closure, 52-
53

  via tree splitting, 52-53, 57

Case features. *See* Features (Case
Features)

Case-checking feature

  complexes for, 62, 75-76, 78-
79, 82-83, 86-88, 107, 113

checking domain for, 62, 76,
78-80, 82-83, 87-88, 107,
113

checking of, 5, 9, 45, 48, 53,
55-60, 62-63, 75-76, 78-80,
82-83, 86-88, 93, 107, 109,
110, 112-114, 117

  by Attract. *See* Attract for
Case Checking

  by covert movement. *See*
Covert Movement for Case
Checking

  by movement (general). *See*
Movement (general) for
Case Checking

  by overt movement. *See* Overt
Movement for Case
Checking

distributional restrictions on, 2,
4, 45-47, 49-53, 55, 58, 60,
62, 75-76, 79, 81-82, 84, 93.
See Also Arguments

as host for complex feature
[POL]-[Q], 108, 110
in colloquial Russian, 98
in dubious Yes/No questions,
100, 102, 112
in embedded Yes/No questions,
98
in emotionally-charged Yes/No
questions, 102, 112
in focal interrogation, 104-105
in presumptive Yes/No
questions, 101-102, 112
in purely informative Yes/No
questions, 99-100, 102, 112
in rhetorical Yes/No questions,
100, 102, 112
non-overt equivalent of, 110
Intransitive Verbs. *See* Verbs
Intrinsic Features. *See* Features
Italian, 42-43, 117
checking of Negative Feature
[NEG] on negative
constituents in non-negative
polarity contexts, 42
differences between English and
Italian, 42
negative concord, 2, 20-21, 35-
37, 39-44
negative constituents, 2, 20-23,
36, 39-42, 44
negative marker *non*, 20, 36,
39-42. *See Also* Negative
Markers and Negative
Concord patterns
as Spec of NegP, 40-41
merging of, 40-41

—J—

Jakobson, 50

—K—

Kiklevič, 23
King, 25, 50, 95, 104
Klenin, 114, 115
Křížková, 38

—L—

Ladusaw, 1-2, 20-22, 31- 32, 35,
37
Laka, 1-2, 19, 22, 32, 77
Larson, 52, 56, 58, 60, 72
Lasnik. *See* Chomsky and Lasnik,
Lasnik and Uriagereka
Lasnik and Uriagereka, 6
Last Resort. *See* Constraints on
Move/Attract
Lexical Functional Grammar, 51
li. See Interrogative particle *li*
Linebarger, 22
Logical Form
and binding, 65
and features, 8, 13, 16, 66, 75,
106
and identification of polarity
feature [POL], 111
and lowering, 57
and reconstruction, 34
and Spell-Out, 8
as level of derivation in
Minimalism, 7
as level of derivation in REST, 7

—M—

Maximal Projections, 9-12, 15,
28, 61. *See Also* Zero-Level
Categories
McCarthy, 106
Merge
as Minimalist operation, 7-8,
10-11, 15
of arguments and Θ-role
assignment, 64-65
of Aspect, 65, 68, 74, 77-78, 83
of English negative marker
n't/not, 42
of functional categories, 71, 80,
83
of Italian negative marker *non*,
40-41
of Negation, 77, 79, 83
of Tense, 66, 69, 74, 79, 80, 83

ordering of with respect to
Move, 67
Mester, 106
Minimal Domain, 15-16, 67, 69
and Attract, 15
and chains, 15
Minimal Link Condition. *See*
Constraints on Move/Attract
Minimal Projection, 10
Minimalist Program, 5-7, 9, 10-
12, 15-18, 24, 26, 29, 30, 32,
35, 44, 49, 53, 56, 60, 63, 66-
68, 72, 76, 91, 97, 105, 109,
113, 117. *See Also* Attract,
Merge, Move, Movement
(general) and the Minimalist
Program, Select
Mismatch. *See* Feature Mismatch
Move, 66. *See Also* Covert
Movement, Movement
(general), Overt Movement
and Equidistance, 15
and Last Resort, 14
and non-matching features, 14
and visibility of traces, 16
as Minimalist operation, 10-12,
14
ordering of with respect to
Merge, 67
Movement (general), 43. *See Also*
Covert Movement, Move, Overt
Movement, WH-movement
and economy considerations, 6,
8, 11, 26
and feature mismatch, 14, 70
and identification of Polarity
Feature [POL], 111
and NEG-absorption, 31-32
and the Government
Transparency Corollary, 59
and the Minimalist Program, 29,
91
constraints on
Equidistance, 15-16, 69, 81.
See Also c-command,
Chains, Traces
Last Resort, 14-15
Minimal Link Condition, 15.
See Also Closeness

for Case checking, 26, 52, 58,
67, 90. *See Also* Covert
Movement for Case
Checking, Overt Movement
for Case Checking
Accusative, 58, 65-66, 69, 79
Genitive of Negation, 59, 78,
83, 87
Nominative, 66-68, 69, 71,
73, 79-80, 83, 88
for feature checking, 8, 13, 29,
62. *See Also* Covert
Movement for Feature
Checking, Overt Movement
for Feature Checking
of Φ-features, 67-68, 71, 79,
80-81, 83-84, 88
of negative feature [NEG], 26-
27, 113
of [WH]-feature, 27
of Neg to C and expletive
negation, 97-98, 103-105,
108-112
verb raising, 59, 61, 65-66, 68-
71, 74, 77-80, 83-84, 87, 88,
92, 107, 116
Mustajoki, 4, 45, 49, 50. *See Also*
Mustajoki and Heino
Mustajoki and Heino, 45, 50, 95

—N—

n't/not, 42-43. *See Also* Negative
Markers and Negative Concord
patterns
as Spec of NegP, 42
merging of, 42
ne (Old Church Slavonic), 2, 38-
39. *See Also* Negative Markers
and Negative Concord patterns
as head or Spec of NegP, 43
ne (Old Russian), 2, 38-39. *See
Also* Negative Markers and
Negative Concord patterns
as head or Spec of NegP, 43
ne (Russian), 2, 19, 39-40. *See
Also* Movement of Neg to C),
Negative Markers
as head of NegP, 25, 35, 39, 43,
59, 113, 115

Movement for Feature
Checking of [NEG],
Movement (general) for
Feature Checking of [NEG],
Overt Movement of
Negative Constituents
of negative constituents, 29-30,
33-34, 39-43, 92, 106, 108.
See Also Covert Movement
for Feature Checking of [NEG],
Negative Constituents
(Preverbal), Overt Movement
for Feature Checking of [NEG]

—P—

Padučeva, 114
Parsons, 33
Partitive, 114, 117
and negation operator, 114
and null quantifier
identification of by partitive
feature [+Qu], 114-115
and Yes/No Questions, 116
highly restricted, 115
licensed by
Interrogative Feature [Q], 117
Negative Feature [NEG], 116-
117
null quantifier, 114
[+Pf] Aspect, 117
partitive feature [+Qu]. *See*
Features
Passive Verbs. *See* Verbs
Pesetsky, 50-51, 114
Phonological Features. *See*
Features
Phonological Form, 111
and features, 8
and pied-piping, 12
and quirky Case marking, 62
as level of derivation in
Minimalism, 7
as level of derivation in REST, 7
Pied-piping, 12, 30
Piñon, 95
poka ne, 3, 94-95. *See Also*
Expletive Negation (Canonical)

Polarity Environments, 21-22,
103, 105. *See Also* Yes/No
Questions
non-strict
and negative constituents, 21-
22, 42
Polarity Feature [POL]. *See* Features
Polarity Phrase. *See* Functional
Categories
Polish, 52
Pollock, 25
Positive Implicature. *See*
Implicature
Postverbal Negative Constituents.
See Negative Constituents
Predicate Feature [PRED]. *See*
Features
Presumptive Yes/No Questions. *See*
Yes/No Questions
Presuppositional Interpretation.
See Also Existential
Interpretation, Generic
Interpretation
and ACC-marked arguments, 48,
57, 75, 89-90, 93
and Genitive of Negation, 85,
86, 90
and NOM-marked arguments, 48-
50, 58, 85, 89-90, 92-93
and tree splitting, 57-58, 90-92,
93
Preverbal Negative Constituents.
See Negative Constituents
Principles and Parameters Theory,
6
PRO, 54-55
Procrastinate, 8
Progovac, 1, 19, 22
Prosodic Inversion
and interrogative particle *li*, 111
Purely Informative Yes/No
Questions. *See* Yes/No
Questions

—Q—

Quirky Case, 62. *See Also* Genitive
of Negation

—R—

purely informative, 98- 100,
103-104
   and expletive negation, 99,
      102-103, 112
   use of *li*, 99-100, 102, 112
rhetorical, 98, 100
   and expletive negation, 102,
      112
   use of *li*, 100, 102, 112

—Z—

Zanuttini, 1-2, 19, 22, 31, 40. *See
Also* Haegeman and Zanuttini
Zero-Level Categories, 11, 15
   as maximal projections, 11-12,
      15, 28, 41, 61-62, 87